HELP ON TH

Help on the Way

A GUIDE TO PERSONAL PRAYER

Josephine Bax

LYNX

First published in Great Britain 1997
Lynx Communications
Society for Promoting Christian Knowledge
Holy Trinity Church
Marylebone Road
London NW1 4DU

British Library Cataloguing-in-Publication Data
A catalogue record of this book is available from the British Library

ISBN 1 901443 01 9

Typeset by David Gregson Associates, Beccles, Suffolk
Printed in Great Britain by The Cromwell Press, Melksham, Wiltshire

Contents

Preface vii
August Night ix

Part 1 Preparing to Pray 1

1 Finding Time for God 3
2 Finding Space for God 7
3 Focusing on God 13

Part 2 Approaching God 17

4 Come to the Father 19
5 Through the Son 23
6 By the Power of the Holy Spirit 27
7 Inviting God in 33
8 Listening to God 36
9 Learning to be Oneself 41

Part 3 Different Kinds of Prayer 45

10 Petition 47
11 Intercession 52
12 Praise 56
13 Saying 'Sorry' 60
14 Thanksgiving 64
15 Prayer of the Heart 66
16 Contemplation 71
17 Praying in the Spirit 75
18 Praying with the Hands 78
19 Mystical Prayer 81
20 Praying with Others 84
21 Worship 86

Epilogue: Spiritual Direction 90

Notes 92

PREFACE

From the moment we are baptized, we enter into a new relationship with God. We embark on a spiritual journey with him, that will last for our entire life, and into the life to come. But we all need help on the way; particularly we need to learn how to pray, because it is our prayer life that will help to sustain this precious relationship with God, and will enable that relationship to grow and develop. Nothing in life is more important than this; the rest of our life hangs upon it. Our prayer life needs to deepen if we are to grow into that person and that life that God has dreamed for us from the beginning, something much better than we could dream for ourselves.

This book aims to give you some help on the way, both with the relationship to God and the prayer that sustains it. It consists of twenty-two sessions. It is not meant to be read straight through, but worked at session by session with the exercises at the end of each part, so that what is suggested becomes part of your everyday prayer life. By the time you have worked your way through the book you should have a knowledge of the basics of prayer, but it is a lifetime's work to develop them and to know not only God, but yourself and how to pray in your own way. It is the simplest and most basic things that we need to come back to again and again as our prayer life develops.

A nun who was celebrating her jubilee – that is fifty years as a nun – looked at a book on prayer by Archbishop Anthony Bloom. She slipped it open at the page entitled 'Prayer for Beginners', and exclaimed, 'Prayer for Beginners – that is good for me also, one can always begin!' We are all beginners when it comes to prayer, and no matter how much we stumble and fall we can always begin again with God.

I pray that those who use this book may be helped to deepen their prayer life and their relationship with God so that they may be filled with his love, peace and joy.

My grateful thanks to Pat Southway, for typing the manuscript for me, and to Sister Angela Helen CSF, for reading it and making helpful suggestions.

Josephine Bax

AUGUST NIGHT

The stars of the Plough
Shine brightly through my bedroom window.
Above them a myriad of stars,
More than I can name or number,
Pierce the darkness of the night sky.
In the north-east a shooting star
Falls to the earth, burning as it is consumed.

This stunning view of God's creation
Fills my heart with awe and wonder.
Though farther off than one can imagine,
These stars are just at the beginning of space.
Beyond them clusters of stars
More than anyone can name or number
Stretch without end into the great unknown.

Below them lies my familiar Earth.
A screech owl calls within the valley.
On the far hill the cars speed westward,
Their headlights pressing the soft darkness,
While on the horizon, a red beacon glows,
And farther round, glimmering in the dark,
The lights of Glastonbury shine out clear.

Lord, God of the great unknown,
I feel helpless in this night.
How can one reach you, learn to love,
Hope to know you, understand you,
Lost as we are in the vastness of space?
My mind is awestruck, overwhelmed,
At creation's power and might displayed.

Yet I think I know you, Lord.
You do not leave us comfortless.
You are also a down-to-earth God.
You draw alongside, revealing yourself
In the familiar, everyday, close-to-home round,

And you make yourself known to us,
As we meet to break the bread.

Help me to receive from you
All that you wish to give me now.
Help me to understand from you
All it is that you wish to reveal.
For I know in part, and understand in part,
And my heart burns within me
As you speak with me on my earthbound way.

Part 1
Preparing to Pray

1

FINDING TIME FOR GOD

God is continuously calling us into relationship with himself. Everything to do with that relationship we describe as spirituality, and prayer is the way in which we communicate with him. Like any relationship, if it is to grow and develop, we need to set aside time to be with him and give him our full attention. This is both the most simple and yet the most difficult thing that we have to do, because we are all so busy these days. 'Can't spend time dreaming about when there is all this work to be done,' said one Christian about his prayer life. But if we don't spend time with God in prayer, he cannot enter our lives and bless them as he is longing to do. We need to come into conscious contact with him before all else; that is the most important work that we can do. He is in all of our life, but we need to give our first attention to him. This must be prime time, not just snatched moments in between other things when we think that we can spare time, or when we are really too tired to pray, because prayer demands energy of us.

People are divided biologically into owls and larks, those who are at their peak in the evening, and those who are at their best in the morning. Apparently it has to do with whether your temperature is highest in the morning or the evening. If you are a lark, then you need to pray first thing in the morning, and for many of us this means getting up early before the rest of the family are around. It is worth the effort. A friend of mine who does this says that it is the best hour of the whole day. If you are an owl you need to pray in the evening, but make sure that you can do this when and where you won't be disturbed.

How much time you spend depends on what you are used to. If you are not used to daily prayer, start by putting a quarter of an hour aside and then gradually increase it by five minutes at a time as you get used to the concentration required. If you are going to do even some of the things that are suggested in this book you are going to need one hour, but don't jump into the deep end straightaway! It is rather like learning to swim – first you have to learn to take your feet off the bottom and let the water hold you up while you do a few strokes. With practice, the few strokes can lengthen until you can swim the width of the swimming pool, but it takes more practice before you can swim the whole length. So it is with prayer. First of all, you have to learn to trust that God is there and listening to your prayer and let the Holy Spirit guide you into speaking with him. Then it is a matter of practice as to how long you can maintain the concentration necessary. With practice you can gradually pray with full attention for longer. But the time also includes the preparation. Archbishop Michael Ramsay – when asked how long he had prayed for that day – said, 'Five minutes, but it took forty minutes to get there!'

Whenever you pray, the important thing is to have a regular, daily discipline. We are called to be disciples of Jesus, and a regular discipline of prayer is a vital part of the discipling. Your time of prayer is your main spiritual meal of the day, and regular meals that are not rushed are essential for a healthy spiritual life. You need to pray whether you feel like it or not, whether you seem at the time to get anything out of it or not. Sometimes you will feel the presence of God, but mostly not, though he is always there. Sometimes it will be easier to pray; sometimes you will encounter doubts and distractions. Sometimes it will be a struggle, at other times an oasis of peace. If you persevere, however, you will find over a period of time that you are changing, that you are becoming more peaceful, that life is more harmonious, that you are becoming conscious of God in the whole of your life.

Nothing is more rewarding than regular time spent in prayer, because it affects everything else, bringing your life into a fulfilling whole under the gentle rule of God.

How are you to spend the time that you have put aside? The rest of this book explores this, but start with this exercise, which is a form of Bible study leading into prayer. It focuses our mind on God, helps us to pray to him, and opens the way for him to speak to us.

Exercises

- Ask God to speak to you through the biblical passage and to help you to pray.

As Jesus and his disciples were on their way, he came to a village where a woman named Martha opened her home to him. She had a sister called Mary, who sat at the Lord's feet listening to what he said. But Martha was distracted by all the preparations that had to be made. She came to him and asked, 'Lord, don't you care that my sister has left me to do all the work by myself? Tell her to help me!' 'Martha, Martha,' the Lord answered, 'you are worried and upset about many things, but only one thing is needed. Mary has chosen what is better, and it will not be taken away from her.'

(Luke 10.38–42)

- Read the Bible passage slowly, chewing it over and entering into the story. What was it like to be Martha, with such an influx of visitors to look after, and no one to help? What was it like to be Mary, sitting at Jesus' feet, drinking in everything that he said and did? Are you Martha, or Mary, or both? What does Jesus mean by 'only one thing is needed?' This may be a reference to Psalm 27.4: 'One thing I ask of the Lord, this is what I seek: that I may dwell in the house of the Lord all the days of my life, to gaze upon the beauty of the Lord and to seek him in his temple.' What is God saying to you through this story?
- Look at the illustration by Vermeer, *Jesus at the home of Martha and Mary*, on the cover of this book. What does the posture of each of the three people mean? And what is the painter saying to us about this story?
- Speak to God about the biblical passages and what they are saying to you.
- Plan how you are going to spend time regularly with God.
- Sit in silence as though at the feet of Jesus, as Mary did, and focus your attention on him. If your mind wanders, look at the illustration and let it bring you back to the presence of Jesus, who is with you, whether you feel it or not.

A prayer for help in prayer:

Lord, without your help I cannot pray,
Please pray in me and for me
That I may come to know and love you better,
And praise and worship you as you deserve.
Amen

A prayer for help in the use of time

Lord, you are from everlasting to everlasting,
But I am trapped in time.
Help me to use this time
According to your perfect will,
So that I may live the life of your kingdom
Which will last for all time and beyond it.
Amen

2

FINDING SPACE FOR GOD

As well as a time to pray during the day, you need a place to withdraw to – what the Russian Orthodox call a '*poustinia*', or hermitage, where no one will disturb you. It needs to be warm and comfortable, so that you are not distracted. The place where you pray will in time become soaked in prayer and easier to pray in. Maybe there is a room in your house where you can pray undisturbed by the family, or in a church nearby that is open during the day, or in the summer a place in the garden where you can get away from it all.

John Wesley, the father of Methodism, was part of a large family, and when his mother wanted to pray, she put her apron over her head, which was a sign that the family must not disturb her! If you are a commuter by train, you could use the time in the train to pray. There is usually a tacit understanding that one doesn't talk. If not, you can close your eyes and your fellow passengers will think that you are having a snooze and will not disturb you! If you drive in to work by car, perhaps there is a church nearby that you can pop into during your lunch hour.

Jesus said, 'When you pray, go into your room, close the door and pray to your Father, who is unseen. Then your Father, who sees what is done in secret, will reward you.'[1] Jesus himself often withdrew to a solitary place, though he was not always successful in getting away from the crowds who followed him everywhere. So choose a place to be a *poustinia*, your space for prayer, and make sure that it is a place where you will not be interrupted.

Jesus then goes on to say how you are to pray: 'When you pray, do not keep on babbling like pagans, for they think they will be heard because of their many words. Do not be like them, for your Father knows what you need before you ask him.'[2]

This is a piece of much-needed advice. It is easy to let off steam to God about everything that concerns us at the moment, and there is a place for that; but we need to leave space for God in our prayers, not besiege him with shopping lists. He knows what is needed better than we do. Instead, Jesus gives us as a model the Lord's Prayer, which is not just a prayer to say, but a guide to prayer in itself. Jesus said,

> *Our Father in heaven,*
> *hallowed be your name,*
> *your kingdom come,*
> *your will be done*
> *on earth as it is in heaven.*
> *Give us today our daily bread.*
> *Forgive us our debts,*
> *as we also have forgiven our debtors.*
> *And lead us not into temptation,*
> *but deliver us from the evil one.*
> (*Matthew 6.9–13*)

This prayer starts with an assumption that is Jesus' unique insight: that God is a loving, heavenly Father, who wants to draw us into an intimate relationship with himself. Therefore our prayer needs to be intimate, loving, trustful. The Aramaic word that is used here means 'Daddy', the word used by a small child for its father. For those who have difficulty in identifying with God as Father, because of unsatisfactory relationships with their own parents, the reminder is here that God is a heavenly Father, a divine parent without the faults of our human parents. If you have not known the love of an earthly father, ask God to show you his divine parenthood, to make up for what you have missed.

In our baptism we were adopted into God's family as his child, not just his creature; and we therefore have the right to call God 'Our Father'. You will notice that it is 'our' and 'us' all the way through, not 'me' and 'my'. This is not an individualistic prayer, but a prayer on behalf of one's community. When we stand before God in prayer, we do so not just on our behalf, but on behalf of the society that we belong to. 'No man is an Island' is the message behind the pronouns. So when we pray we need to remember that we are representing not just ourselves, but our family, our Christian community, and the wider community within which we are set.

When we pray, we need to revere God and all that he stands for, so Jesus tells us to pray 'Hallowed be your name'. The name of a person in biblical times told you about the sort of person they were, so God's name tells us something of what he is, and what he stands for. The name 'Jesus' derives from the same Aramaic root as the name 'Joshua', and means 'saviour' or 'deliverer'. Many people today use

God's name only as a swear word. Jesus tells us on the contrary to respect and revere the name of God, which is something of what 'hallowed' means, though it means more than that – 'make holy, consecrate, set apart'. When we approach God in prayer therefore, we need to come being conscious that he is a holy God who deserves our reverence.

Jesus also tells us to pray that God's will be done and his kingdom come on earth as it is in heaven. There is a sense in which all our prayer should be an aligning of ourselves with the will of God. Sometimes this is easy; sometimes it is hard, as Jesus found in Gethsemane when faced with the cross; but it is only as God's will is done that his just and gentle rule is established here on earth as it is in heaven. Heaven, and God's kingdom, are simply where God's will is done, and when we can say our 'Yes' to God's will, his love and joy and peace will be established in our hearts, whatever our circumstances.

The whole of the first half of the Lord's Prayer is thus about God, his nature, and how we should approach him. But Jesus does not forget us and our needs. The rest of the prayer is about us. 'Give us today all we need for the day.' Jesus tells us to live a day at a time, and not to take on more than that day requires. So much of our time is taken up by worrying about the future, or thinking about the past, but we are to live in the now, in the present, relying on God's providence a day at a time.

'Daily bread' too is basic. It is about needs, not wants; enough to keep us going, not to satisfy all our aspirations. It also presumes that everything we have comes from God. Today so many people feel self-sufficient; they are managing OK, but what we really need to have is a daily dependence upon God. God knows our needs before we ask, Jesus says, and 'daily bread' represents all that we need to live on this day as God requires.

The next portion of the prayer is about the need for forgiveness. The NIV Bible talks about forgiving debts; other translations about forgiving sins, or forgiving trespasses. We are all fallible human beings, in need of daily forgiveness. We need to be forgiven, and we also need to forgive others. One of the commonest reasons for people to stumble in the Christian life is because of not forgiving others. Some people ask for forgiveness for themselves, but are full of resentment about what so-and-so has done! Jesus is so concerned about this that he puts a gloss at the end of the Lord's Prayer like this: 'For if you forgive men when they sin against you, your heavenly Father will also forgive you. But if you do not forgive men their sins, your Father will not forgive your sins.'[3]

Elsewhere he is reported as saying: 'And when you stand praying, if you hold anything against anyone, forgive him, so that your Father in heaven may forgive your sins.'[4] In other words, we must drop all resentments, whether they are justified or not, when we come to pray; otherwise our prayers will be rejected. This is easier said than done. We cannot help our feelings, but we can be willing to forgive, and that is asked of us if our own sins are to be forgiven. This is a priority if we are to lead a life of prayer, and needs stressing.

The prayer ends, 'Lead us not into temptation, but deliver us from the evil one.' One modern translation reads, 'do not put us to the test'. Many people have found it difficult to believe that God will deliberately lead us into temptation, but the fact is that we are frequently tested, not necessarily because God is putting us through it, but because of our own desires and inclinations. He allows us to be tested, but will not allow us to be tested beyond our endurance. He makes a way of escape so that we can endure it. St Paul says: 'No temptation has seized you except what is common to man. And God is faithful; he will not let you be tempted beyond what you can bear. But when you are tempted, he will also provide a way out so that you can stand up under it.'[5]

So we pray for release from temptation, and deliverance from the evil one, or from evil. Many people today do not believe in the personification of evil, but rather in a vague force, or perhaps just our own faults. Those who wish to deepen their prayer life will, however, come at some stage into conflict with Satan, the evil one, who does not like to see us so close to the kingdom of heaven. There is a spiritual struggle going on in the heavenly realms, and to pray is to become engaged in that struggle, so do not be surprised if you sometimes have to battle to pray.

There are three mistakes that are commonly made about the power of evil. The first is to fear the power of evil, or become obsessed by it. We do not have to live in fear of the power of evil, because Christ has overcome the evil one on the cross, and we can live in the power of his victory. In his name, Jesus, and by the power of the cross we can bind and rebuke Satan, and tell him where to go, and he will have to obey.

Another mistake is to disregard the power of evil, or disbelieve in it, and behave as we like, thinking all will automatically be well. St Paul says: 'So, if you think you are standing firm, be careful that you don't fall!'[6] We must not stand in our own strength, or battle with Satan except by the power and authority of Jesus, which as Christians we can claim.

The third mistake is to lay ourselves open to the power of evil by indulging in occultism or spiritualism, which many young people do now out of curiosity. The Church has always condemned such practices because of the danger they can put us into through the interference of the power of evil. To take part in such practices is a matter for repentance, and if they cause difficulties, help should be sought from a Christian minister who is experienced in such matters. For those who are following Christ faithfully, however, there is no need to fear, but there is a need to be wary of this whole area because of our own weakness.

Many Christians put a gloss on the end of this prayer: 'For the kingdom, the power and the glory are yours, now and for ever. Amen.' This fixes our eyes back on God; on his power and glory which is eternal. It brings us back from ourselves, and from the power of evil to looking at God, and glorifying him as we need to do if we come to prayer. We must not look down at ourselves and our problems so much as we look up at God, who holds all things in his hands. In our prayers as in our daily practice, we need to make space for God.

Exercises

- Read Matthew 6.6–15 again slowly, thinking about what is being said and praying to God about anything that particularly strikes you. Finish by saying the Lord's Prayer.
- Paraphrase the Lord's Prayer in your own words, without losing the original meaning. We know the Lord's Prayer so well that it is easy to say it without paying attention to the meaning, but this will help you to do so.
- Search your mind to know whether there is anyone who you still feel resentment towards, either in your past life or nowadays. If there is anyone, say the following prayer:

  Thank you, Lord, for winning forgiveness of my sins on the cross. Thank you for your mercy and love towards me. I unconditionally forgive all who have offended me, all who have failed in love towards me, all who have injured me in any way. I pray that God will also forgive their sins, through Jesus Christ our Lord. Amen.

- Search your mind to know whether at any time in the past, (perhaps as a child or a teenager) you have in any way dabbled in occultism or spiritualism (such as playing with Ouija boards or table-rapping). If so, ask God's forgiveness for this, and whether you have done so or not, say the following prayer for protection:

  Thank you, Lord, for overcoming the power of evil on the cross. Thank you that we can live in the power of that victory. I pray now in your name, Jesus, for protection for myself, my family, my friends and neighbours, and all who I meet with. In Jesus' name I bind Satan, and tell him to go where he belongs, and not to trouble us. Help us, Lord, to live in your victory for us on the cross, to resist temptation, and to reject all that is evil, for your name's sake and for your glory. Amen.

- Find a place to be your *poustinia*, where you can withdraw to be alone with God.
- A prayer for space for God, and space to be with God:

  Heavenly Father, you deserve the first place in my life.
  Help me to find space to be with you, and space for you in my prayers,
  So that you may play your proper place in my life
  In Jesus' name I ask it,

  Amen

3

FOCUSING ON GOD

Having set aside the time to pray, and a place to pray, the next thing we need to do is to focus the mind on God. We need help to do this; otherwise the mind will wander here, there and everywhere, on to what are called 'distractions'. Do not worry if you find your mind going off course or if you encounter distractions in prayer. We all suffer from these from time to time. The thing to do is to have something to help you focus on God, and to bring your mind back to God when it does wander.

The way most people use to prepare themselves to pray is meditation. It is important to realize that meditation is not an end in itself, but a way into prayer. We meditate so that we can pray, not the other way around. 'Meditation' is a blanket word that means different things to different people.

The different schools of prayer have different ways of meditating. If you are a Benedictine using Scripture as your base for meditation, you will think about it and study it in an intellectual way. If you are a Carmelite, you will not think about it, but try in your meditation to get to a deeper level than words, where God communicates to us in silence, speaks without speaking, and you will focus on Jesus, but without trying to fix a picture in your mind. If you use what St Ignatius called 'imaginative contemplation', you will use pictures to help you fix your mind upon God, and your feelings will be important. Which kind of meditation you will find most helpful will depend on your gifts and temperament. If you are predominantly a thinker, you will follow the Benedictine way. If you are an intuitive and a natural contemplative you will not necessarily need words. If you have a visual imagination, you will find the way that many people have been introduced to by St Ignatius helpful.

Another way of meditation is to use Christian symbols. If you meditate and pray in a church, there will be plenty of symbols to use. At home you can use a cross, a candle, water, bread or wine to help you focus. If you are a person to whom symbol speaks strongly, this form of meditation will suit you.

Yet another way is to use an object of God's creation to draw near to its Maker. It is important to realize that we worship the Creator, not his creation, and this is what sets Christians on a different course to the New Age movement. However, God has set his stamp on everything he has made, and creation can show us something about the God who has made it. St Francis got it right in his wonderful hymn, 'All creatures of our God and king', when he calls on all creation to join us in worshipping the Holy Trinity.

What I am describing is Christian meditation: meditation that uses Scripture, or Christian images, or God's creation to lead us by the Holy Spirit, through Jesus to the Father. This is quite different from Eastern meditation, which leads us into the self and leaves us there. This is called 'entasis', whereas Christian meditation is 'extasis'; it leads us outwards to God and to our neighbour. These forms of emphasis are fundamentally different, and it is important to realize that yoga and Eastern forms of meditation are not for Christians to use. We have a great variety of our own forms which lead us along the Christian path more effectively.

When we meditate, we need to ask God the Holy Spirit to lead and guide us. We can only understand spiritual things through the action of the Holy Spirit himself. As St Paul says:

> The Spirit searches all things, even the deep things of God. For who among men knows the thoughts of a man except the man's spirit within him? In the same way no-one knows the thoughts of God except the Spirit of God. We have not received the spirit of the world but the Spirit who is from God, that we may understand what God has freely given us. This is what we speak, not in words taught us by human wisdom but in words taught by the Spirit, expressing spiritual truths in spiritual words. The man without the Spirit does not accept the things that come from the Spirit of God, for they are foolishness to him, and he cannot understand them, because they are spiritually discerned.
>
> (1 Corinthians 2.10–14)

So, as we embark on our journey, we ask the Holy Spirit to come with us as guide, navigator, teacher and friend, and this he will do as it is his task to show us the Father and the Son, and to help us pray.

(There are a variety of different kinds of meditation at the end of this section. Do not be put off if you find any of them difficult at first. They all come more easily with practice.)

A prayer for God's guidance

Come, Holy Spirit,
Set our hearts on fire with your love.
Guide and help us in our meditation and our prayers
And teach us the eternal truths of God.
For Christ's sake we ask it.

Amen

The first kind of meditation is using Scripture to focus our mind on God. Use the following Scripture in two different ways and discover whether you are a Benedictine or an Ignatian!

> Now Moses was tending the flock of Jethro his father-in-law, the priest of Midian, and he led the flock to the far side of the desert and came to Horeb, the mountain of God. There the angel of the Lord appeared to him in flames of fire from within a bush. Moses saw that though the bush was on fire it did not burn up. So Moses thought, 'I will go over and see this strange sight – why the bush does not burn up.'
>
> When the Lord saw that he had gone over to look, God called to him from within the bush, 'Moses! Moses!' And Moses said, 'Here I am.'
>
> 'Do not come any closer', God said. 'Take off your sandals, for the place where you are standing is holy ground.' Then he said, 'I am the God of your father, the God of Abraham, the God of Isaac and the God of Jacob.' At this Moses hid his face, because he was afraid to look at God. (Exodus 3.1–6)

Exercises

- Read the passage slowly. Stop if anything strikes you and think it through. Ask yourself the following questions: What has to happen before God calls Moses? What does God disclose about himself? What does this passage say to you about your own relationship with God? End with praying to God about that.
- Imagine yourself in this scene in the desert; feel the heat and the dryness. Where are you in the picture? How does it feel? How do you respond to God? How does it feel to be Moses? To be called by name? If anything particularly strikes you, stop and pray about it to God.

- Light a candle and read the following words: 'When Jesus spoke again to the people he said, "I am the light of the world. Whoever follows me will never walk in darkness, but will have the light of my life."[1]

  Focus on the candle and ask Jesus to shine his light into you to literally enlighten you. Wait in silence, coming back to the words and the symbol of the candle if your mind wanders. End with the following prayer:

  Thank you, Lord, that you call us into relationship with yourself.
  Thank you that we need not walk in darkness, but can have the light of life.
  Help us to walk in the light of your presence with us,
  Now and always.

  Amen

- Choose a piece of God's creation and meditate on it. Let it speak to you of its Creator. You can use flowers or fruit, but the best thing to use, if you can obtain it, is a seashell. It is tactile, you can handle it, and the tropical seashells you can buy are exquisitely beautiful. God has made this wonderful object to protect a humble little mollusc that shuffled along the ocean floor.

Part 2
Approaching God

4

COME TO THE FATHER

How we pray will depend on how we approach God. Who and what we think he is will colour our whole relationship with him, including our prayer life.

The discovery that the Israelites made about God which is mirrored in the Old Testament is that of God's '*hesed*', constant, faithful love. They discovered that God loved them, and that this love was constant. It could be relied upon, so that they would pray to God with reverence, but also with confidence, knowing that he had their best interests at heart.

In the New Testament, God's love is shown to us by sending his beloved Son into the world so that we might live through him.[1] Jesus showed us that God is not only loving, he is love. His love is demonstrated throughout Jesus' life, but most of all in his dying for us on the cross. The discovery that the Israelites made is sharpened into focus in the New Testament, and the nature of God's love is made plain for us. So as Christians we can approach God with confidence and trust, knowing that he has made us in love, for love, and that he himself is love itself.

If you imagine that in prayer you are praying to the most loving and compassionate person you can think of, you will still fall short of the reality. We cannot imagine God's love but we can know it through heart knowledge. All God's creatures know instinctively what love is; even the smallest child responds to it. So we must pray that God by his Holy Spirit will pour his love into our hearts so that we can respond to his love with love and knowledge of the heart.

The nature of the Father's love is explained vividly for us in the parable of the prodigal son, which, as the *NIV Study Bible* says, could better be called the parable of the father's love, because in it the father shows his love for both his sons. Read the parable slowly, and allow it to tell you the nature of the Father's love.

> Jesus continued: 'There was a man who had two sons. The younger one said to his father, 'Father, give me my share of the estate.' So he divided his property between them.

Not long after that, the younger son got together all he had, set off for a distant country and there squandered his wealth in wild living. After he had spent everything, there was a severe famine in that whole country, and he began to be in need. So he went and hired himself out to a citizen of that country, who sent him to his fields to feed pigs. He longed to fill his stomach with the pods that the pigs were eating, but no-one gave him anything.

When he came to his senses, he said, 'How many of my father's hired men have food to spare, and here I am starving to death! I will set out and go back to my father and say to him: 'Father, I have sinned against heaven and against you. I am no longer worthy to be called your son; make me like one of your hired men.' So he got up and went to his father.

But while he was still a long way off, his Father saw him and was filled with compassion for him; he ran to his son, threw his arms around him and kissed him.

The son said to him, 'Father, I have sinned against heaven and against you. I am no longer worthy to be called your son.'

But the father said to his servants, 'Quick! Bring the best robe and put it on him. Put a ring on his finger and sandals on his feet. Bring the fattened calf and kill it. Let's have a feast and celebrate. For this son of mine was dead and is alive again; he was lost and is found.' So they began to celebrate.

Meanwhile, the older son was in the field. When he came near the house, he heard music and dancing. So he called one of the servants and asked him what was going on. 'Your brother has come,' he replied, 'and your father has killed the fattened calf because he has him back safe and sound.'

The older brother became angry and refused to go in. So his father went out and pleaded with him. But he answered his father, 'Look! All these years I've been slaving for you and never disobeyed your orders. Yet you never gave me even a young goat so I could celebrate with my friends. But when this son of yours who has squandered your property with prostitutes comes home, you kill the fattened calf for him!'

'My son,' the father said, 'you are always with me, and everything I have is yours. But we had to celebrate and be glad, because this brother of yours was dead and is alive again; he was lost and is found.'

(Luke 15.11–32)

Exercises

- Write down all the adjectives you can think of to describe the nature of the Father as shown by this parable.
- Write down all the adjectives you can think of to describe the elder brother as shown in this parable.
- Compare the two lists. Many people think that God is like the elder brother – judgemental and rejecting – so they do not approach God with love and confidence. Jesus is telling us the opposite in this story.
- What does this story tell you about how you can approach God? What is its significance for your prayer life?
- The epistles of St John are full of meditations about God's love. Here is an extract for you to meditate on.

Dear friends, let us love one another, for love comes from God. Everyone who loves has been born of God and knows God. Whoever does not love does not know God, because God is love. This is how God showed his love among us: He sent his one and only Son . . . as an atoning sacrifice for our sins. Dear friends, since God so loved us, we also ought to love one another. No-one has ever seen God; but if we love each other, God lives in us and his love is made complete in us. (1 John 4.7–12)

A Prayer for God's Love

Thank you, heavenly Father, for your constant love.
Thank you, Jesus, for loving us and laying down your life for us.
Holy Spirit, please pour your love into our hearts,
So that we may know God's love for us,
And respond with love and thanksgiving,
Now and always.

Amen

Dawn

Back go the curtains.
The valley lies before me.
The lights are on at the farm.
In the distance the speeding lights
Of the main road
Tell of ceaseless movement.
My neighbour's lights are on.
From the chimney the smoke curls
As the fire is drawn up.
Under the bare trees
The last of the apples lie untouched,
As the relentless round of the season
Takes us towards Christmas.
The leaden sky lightens,
As all around
The trees and fields stand waiting
For the new day.
And I too wait,
For the unknown to become known,
For the silence to speak,
For love to make its entrance
And seal the moment for eternity.

5

THROUGH THE SON

St John's Gospel is full of Jesus' teaching about the Father. All the teaching stresses the oneness of Jesus and the Father. Here are a few excerpts:

'The Father loves the Son and has placed everything in his hands.'[1]

'I tell you the truth, the Son can do nothing by himself; he can do only what he sees his Father doing, because whatever the Father does, the Son also does. For the Father loves the Son and shows him all he does.'[2]

'I and the Father are one.'[3]

The most extended piece of teaching Jesus gives on his relationship to the Father comes in John 14. Here is an extract from it:

> Thomas said to him, 'Lord, we don't know where you are going, so how can we know the way?'
>
> Jesus answered, 'I am the way and the truth and the life. No-one comes to the Father except through me. If you really knew me, you would know my Father as well. From now on, you do know him and have seen him.'
>
> Philip said, 'Lord, show us the Father and that will be enough for us.'
>
> Jesus answered: 'Don't you know me, Philip, even after I have been among you such a long time? Anyone who has seen me has seen the Father. How can you say, "Show us the Father?" Don't you believe that I am in the Father, and that the Father is in me? The words I say to you are not just my own. Rather, it is the Father, living in me, who is doing his work. Believe me when I say that I am in the Father and the Father is in me; or at least believe on the evidence of the miracles themselves. I tell you the truth, anyone who has faith in me will do what I have been doing. He will do even greater things than these, because I am going to the Father. And I will do whatever you ask in my name, so that the Son may bring glory to the Father. You may ask me for anything in my name, and I will do it. (John 14.5–14)

Jesus is here plainly stating that not only is he the way to the Father, but that the only way to the Father is through him. If we wish to make a relationship with God, and particularly if we want to pray to God, we must go through Jesus. He shows us the Father and he brings us to him. If we use Jesus as the focus of our meditation and the focus of our prayer, he will open the way for us to the Father. In Jesus we are acceptable to God the Father through his beloved Son, but if we try to come some other way, we will find our progress barred. We are not acceptable in our own right. We must put on Christ if the Father is to hear and answer our prayers. This means that the phrase 'through Jesus Christ our Lord' that we often find at the end of more formal prayers is not just a deferential phrase, but the whole way in which we must proceed, in our prayer and in our attitude to God. To come to the Father through Jesus Christ our Lord is to open doors in heaven through which doors on earth are opened.

Jesus also says (verse 14) that whatever we ask for in his name he will do. This again doesn't just mean that we stick his name at the end of the prayer, but that we ask according to the character and nature of Jesus. A person's name in the Bible stands for the kind of person they are. Jesus will not do anything out of character just because we ask him for it, but he will do anything that we ask if it is within his nature to do it. For example, if we ask on behalf of a friend that he will bless them with his love and joy and peace, that is the sort of thing that he is about and will do. Especially we should pray for people that God's will may be done in their life. That is a prayer that we can expect to get an answer to. But if we pray for something inappropriate, don't be surprised if the answer is 'No'! God does say 'No' if our prayers are not in line with his nature and his will, which are very different from our point of view at times.

In praying to the Father through the Son we can be confident that the Father will hear us. In coming ourselves to the Father through the Son we can be confident that the Father will receive us. Hebrews 7.25 tells us that Jesus is able to save completely those who come to God through him, because he lives to intercede for them.

What does it mean to 'put on Christ'? It means to come to Jesus in trust and confidence that he has done everything necessary to open the way for us to God. We do not trust in ourselves, and anything we have done or can be, but in what Jesus Christ has done for us on the cross. If we come in that knowledge, and with that attitude, our prayers will be heard. So come to the Father through the Son, if you wish to lead a life of prayer.

Exercises

- Meditate on the passage from John 14.5–14 given earlier in the text and end with this prayer:

  Lord Jesus Christ, Son of the Father,
  May all creation praise you for what you have done on the cross.
  Thank you for making it possible
  To come to the Father through you.
  Beloved Son, we are accepted in you,
  Keep us close to your heart
  And pray for us.
  Hear our prayers and the longings of our hearts
  For your name's sake.

  Amen

- Use a cross or a picture of the cross to help you meditate on what Jesus Christ has done to open the way to the Father. End with your own prayer of thanksgiving and/or the prayer above.
- Read Colossians 1.15–23 and meditate on it. Out of your meditation make your own prayer to Jesus, thanking him for who he is and what he has done. End with the prayer above.

The Supremacy of Christ

He is the image of the invisible God, the firstborn over all creation. For by him all things were created: things in heaven and on earth, visible and invisible, whether thrones or powers or rulers or authorities; all things were created by him and for him. He is before all things, and in him all things hold together. And he is the head of the body, the church; he is the beginning and the firstborn from among the dead, so that in everything he might have the supremacy. For God was pleased to have all his fulness dwell in him, and through him to reconcile to himself all things, whether things on earth or things in heaven, by making peace through his blood, shed on the cross.

Once you were alienated from God and were enemies in your minds because of your evil behaviour. But now he has reconciled you by Christ's physical body through death to present you holy in his sight, without blemish and free from accusation – if you continue in your faith, established and firm, not moved from the hope held out in the gospel. This is the gospel that you heard and that has been proclaimed to every creature under heaven, and of which I, Paul, have become a servant. (Colossians 1.15–23)

Suffering

The tears came unbidden,
Unexpected, out of the blue,
Welling up from a past hurt
Deep in the unconscious.
Why come to the surface now,
Disturbing the tranquil peace
Of this moonlit night?
Why this heartache,
Sharp as a physical pain?
Why this sudden grief and anguish?
Only the suffering and heartbroken God,
Bearing his scars,
Can draw near and understand.
Only the one who bears
The suffering of the whole world
Can touch and heal.
Only the love and compassion
Of him who endured the cross
Can bind the wound,
Heal the memory, and
Restore the stricken one within.
So come Lord Jesus,
And with your scarred hands
Touch the wounded spirit
And make it whole again.
Only the scar will remain
To show where suffering came.
A reminder of him,
The wounded healer,
Who bears our frail humanity.

6

BY THE POWER OF THE HOLY SPIRIT

The word '*Christos*' in Greek means the anointed one. In olden days, kings and queens were anointed with oil, and still are today in the coronation service. This is a symbolic way of expressing the anointing of the Holy Spirit which will empower them in leadership. In the Old Testament only leaders of the people were anointed like this – kings, priests, and prophets – but in the New Testament we find that all who believed in Jesus Christ, that he is the Son of God, were anointed with the Holy Spirit. So today, we Christians are each a little *Christos*. The word 'Christian' means someone who is anointed with the Holy Spirit, which is given to us to empower us to lead the Christian life.

We have free will, however. It is not until we hand over the tiller, so to speak, to the Holy Spirit – until we allow him to be in control of our lives – that he can really do his work in us. We must voluntarily hand over our lives to God the Holy Spirit and allow him to lead us and fill us if we wish to grow as Christians and deepen our prayer life. This is easier said than done, because in many of us there lurks a fear of what God may ask of us. This is why a confident trust in the Father's love, and a belief that he has our best interest at heart, is necessary before we can make progress. There is also in us the desire to dominate, to be in control, and this too needs to be dealt with before we can be in business with God. What is asked of us is that we make an effort of will and of trust in God, that will allow him to lead us according to his will, which will sometimes be what we want, but at other times not. He will not force us against our will, but we need to be humble, obedient and trusting that God our Maker knows better than we do what is best for us in the long run.

And the long run means eternity. That is what God is preparing us for. He wants us to be the person he made us to be, and to do God's will, though hard at times, is to find the ultimate fulfilment and happiness we are all looking for.

If we surrender our lives to God, and allow him to fill us with his Holy Spirit, if we say our 'Yes' to God, not just in a euphoric moment, but in the nitty-gritty of our daily lives, he will help us to pray. He is our best guide to prayer, and he prays in us and for us. When we don't know how and what to pray, the thing to do is to ask the Holy Spirit and he will help us in our difficulties. St Paul says,

> The Spirit helps us in our weakness. We do not know what we ought to pray, but the Spirit himself intercedes for us with groans that words cannot express. And he who searches our hearts knows the mind of the Spirit, because the Spirit intercedes for the saints in accordance with God's will. (Romans 8.26–7)

The Spirit also brings the Scriptures to life and helps us to understand them. He teaches us about the Father and the Son, and brings us to Jesus, in whom we can see the Father. Indeed the sure sign that the Holy Spirit is at work in our lives is whether our love for Jesus is growing. The Holy Spirit is very self-effacing. He does not point to himself, but points us to Jesus, and through him to the Father. It is he who keeps us on the Christian way, and gives us the strength to live it, which we do not have of ourselves. St Paul says, 'Now it is God who makes both us and you stand firm in Christ. He anointed us, set his seal of ownership on us, and put his Spirit in our hearts as a deposit, guaranteeing what is to come.'[1] So the Spirit is not just helping us to pray and live the Christian life now; he is a down payment, a pledge of the greater joy that is to be ours in the future.

If you want to come closer to God, if you want to go deeper in your prayer life, that is a sure sign that the Spirit is already at work in your heart. All you need to do is to give him a free rein in your life, to do what God wants to do to bring you that greater joy. So come to the Father, through the Son, and by the power of the Holy Spirit if you wish to pray and lead a truly Christian life.

Even though we received the Holy Spirit at baptism, we need continually to ask for his refilling of us – because we leak! Here are some prayers and meditations to help you to open yourself more fully to the work of the Holy Spirit.

A Prayer for God's Guidance

Come, Holy Spirit,
Set our hearts on fire with your love.
Guide and help us in our meditation and our prayers
And teach us the eternal truths of God.
For Christ's sake we ask it.

Amen

Exercises

- Begin with the prayer for God's guidance. The Holy Spirit is unseen, but three symbols are used to represent his person: the dove, the fire and the wind. In this first meditation we think of the Holy Spirit as the dove:

Then Jesus came from Galilee to the Jordan to be baptised by John. But John tried to deter him, saying, 'I need to be baptised by you, and do you come to me?'

Jesus replied, 'Let it be so now; it is proper for us to do this to fulfil all righteousness.' Then John consented.

As soon as Jesus was baptised, he went up out of the water. At that moment heaven was opened, and he saw the Spirit of God descending like a dove and lighting on him. And a voice from heaven said, 'This is my Son whom I love; with him I am well pleased.' (Matthew 3.13–17)

Read the passage slowly and stop if anything strikes you. Think it through and pray to God about it. Did Jesus need to be baptized? If so, why? Why do you think the Holy Spirit descended like a dove? What is the significance of being baptized in the Holy Spirit as well as water baptism? End with this prayer:

A Prayer for the Help of the Holy Spirit

Come, Holy Spirit,
Unless you fill us, we are empty.
Unless you teach us, we are ignorant.
Unless you guide us, we will wander.
Come to us, abide with us, fill us.
Help us to know and love the Father and the Son.
We ask this for their glory.

Amen

The Shy Bird

Sitting on the terrace
In the warm summer sun,
I seem to be alone,
But as I watch and wait,
Still and quiet,
Life begins to show
All around me.
At my feet a tiny jenny-wren
Searches the warm stones
For little insects that run
In and out of the drystone wall
On summer days;
While round my head
A gathering of swallows twittering
Wheel and dart through the air,
And come to rest on my roof.
I count more than fifty of them.
A thrilling sight –
Yet it is peaceful to be so close
To their retiring life and shy beauty.
It is like those times
While watching and waiting
Still and quiet,
The shy bird, the Holy Dove,
Comes close.
Only a deep peace
Betrays his presence
And the praise and joy
Rising from the heart
Where he rests;
Which thrills to his presence
Yet rests in him.
You cannot catch him, hold him,
Detain him against his will.
He remains elusive, yet,
When we wait for him and watch,
Still and quiet,
He will come to us.
Unobtrusive, self-effacing,

He points us to the Father and the Son,
Gives us his gifts,
Gives us his love, his joy, his peace.
Only his fruits remain
To show he has been with us.
His hidden life, his shy beauty
Cannot be possessed,
Only cherished and longed for.
So come, Holy Spirit,
Pledge of the Father's love,
Seal of his ownership,
And make us new again.
Bring us to Jesus' feet
And let us stay there,
Waiting and watching,
Still and quiet,
Yet rejoicing to be there
By the strong power
Of this shy bird,
The Holy Dove,
With us now
In this moment of time
That brings us into eternity.

- The Holy Spirit as fire and wind. Read these Bible passages:

When the day of Pentecost came, they were all together in one place. Suddenly a sound like the blowing of a violent wind came from heaven and filled the whole house where they were sitting. They saw what seemed to be tongues of fire that separated and came to rest on each of them. All of them were filled with the Holy Spirit and began to speak in other tongues as the Spirit enabled them. (Acts 2.1–4)

Jesus answered, 'I tell you the truth, unless a man is born of water and the Spirit, he cannot enter the kingdom of God. Flesh gives birth to flesh, but the Spirit gives birth to spirit. You should not be surprised at my saying, 'You must be born again.' The wind blows wherever it pleases ... So it is with everyone born of the Spirit. (John 3.5–8)

Then answer these questions:

a) The wind is unseen, but you can see its effects in the blowing about of objects such as trees. Similarly the Spirit is unseen but you can see his effects. What are they?

b) The Spirit rested on the disciples in the form of flames of fire. What do you think is the meaning of the symbol?

c) The gift of tongues is the gift of a language not known to the speaker. How can this gift be used in prayer?

- Meditate on the three symbols of the Holy Spirit: wind, fire and the dove. End with the prayer for the help of the Holy Spirit.

7

INVITING GOD IN

Here I am! I stand at the door and knock. If anyone hears my voice and opens the door, I will go in and eat with him, and he with me. (Revelation 3.20)

For many people who hear this verse, it conjures up a picture, *The Light of the World* by Holman Hunt, which is in St Paul's Cathedral. This picture shows the figure of Christ, holding a lantern, knocking at a door which remains closed. This verse, on which it is based, is astonishing. It is addressed to the church in Laodicea. Jesus does not say 'I am the head of the Church; you must take notice of what I say.' Instead he waits outside, knocking, asking to be allowed in. It is truly a picture of humility, of God descending to our pride.

It reminds us of two things concerning our relationship with God. First of all, it is God who takes the initiative and asks us to come into relationship with him. If we are seeking for God, it is because he has already found us, and is drawing us to himself. We do not have to plead with him for this relationship; it has already been offered to us.

Second, we are free to accept this relationship or reject it. Although we are God's creation, he has created us as free beings who can turn away from him or, using the picture language of Revelation, we can keep the door bolted and barred. Many people and many churches do this, although they in truth belong to him. Many people go through a kind of spiritual adolescence, like adolescents rebelling against their parents. They go away from God, but like adolescents, as they grow up spiritually they often come back to him at a later stage. Others bolt and bar the door because they are afraid of what God would ask of them or do in their lives. They forget that Christ is not just loving and compassionate and seeks their greater good; he is love itself.

It is love who is knocking at our door, and if we keep him out, it is our loss as much as his. But if we are to lead a life of prayer we need to go deeper into this relationship with him. We must unlock the door and let him in, so that we can eat with him, and he with us, a symbol of our fellowship with him. It is easier said than done. Fear keeps the door bolted and barred, but love wishes to open it, and Christ waits until our trust in him is sufficient for us to let him in. To begin with, the conversation may take place through a chink in the door, but sooner or later we must take the step of inviting God in. The bolts must be drawn by us, and the door opened by us, before the relationship can really develop. It is as simple and as difficult as that. God will not intrude upon our inner lives unless we want him to. He respects us too much for that. His friendship is on offer. Everything depends on how we respond.

The Lord of the Church and the Creator of the universe is waiting for our invitation. Even so, come, Lord Jesus.

Exercises

- Use the verse for meditation, ending with a prayer inviting God in. You can devise your own prayer, or use this one:

Come, Lord Jesus,
Into my heart and home.
You are a welcome guest.
Feast at my table,
Drink of my wine.
Thank you for your friendship.
Please stay with me
Now and always.
Amen.

- Jesus said that as we welcome the least of one of his children, we welcome him. Ask someone to a meal who needs your fellowship, as a sacrament of your fellowship with Christ.

House Communion

The church resists
All attempts to heat it in this cold.
The faithful few who come
To midweek Communion are taking refuge
In my much warmer house today.
My dining-room table
Draped with a 'fair linen cloth'
Doubles for an altar,
The chairs in a horseshoe round it.
The sitting room doubles for a vestry
Warmed by a large log fire.
I draw up the fires,
Get the house ready,
Then sit down to wait.
As I sit and pray,
The *shekinah* glory of the Lord
Falls upon the house
Filling it with his presence.
It is as if he said,
'You can't come to my house,
So I come to yours this day.'

Lord, we will have warmer bodies,
But give us warmer hearts
To receive you now.
Thank you for coming to us.
We come to you,
And ask nothing better
Than your living presence.
May it be so
Now and always.

8

LISTENING TO GOD

All relationships are, or should be, two-way. We give and receive, talk and listen. Our relationship with God is no different. Prayer should not be a monologue from us, but a two-way communication. God can and does speak to us as well as we to him, but not necessarily in words. As well as speaking to God, our prayer should consist of times of waiting on God, giving him space to speak to us in whatever way he chooses.

Archbishop Anthony Bloom talks of this waiting on God as being like a sentry at his post, aware and watchful. Yet we must not strain or be tense as we wait on God. Anthony Bloom tells of a woman who came to him and complained that she never felt the presence of God when she was praying. He told her to sit in her room and knit before the face of God. She tried this and came back to tell him that as she knitted, she became conscious of how nice her room was, and while she was thinking of this, she became aware of the presence of God filling the room. The problem had been that she was straining and tense, but the knitting helped her to relax and enjoy just being alone in God's presence. This relaxed yet aware and concentrated form of waiting and praying is called 'recollection', or 'being recollected'.

God does sometimes speak to us in words, though this needs always to be checked with other Christians whom we trust. A genuine communication from God will always be confirmed in one way or another, though it may take some time. Bishop Hugh Montefiore tells of how one day he had a vision of Jesus. He was a Jew at that time and knew nothing about Jesus, but somehow he knew that this person was Jesus. As he was looking at the vision, the words came to him, 'Follow me.' He responded by becoming a Christian, and eventually a bishop in the Anglican Church. There may not be a vision, but words may come to our minds which can be from God, but which need to be confirmed before any action is taken.

Much more often, God speaks to us through Scripture. The Bible has been described as a love letter from God, and through it God can speak to us. If he is to do so, we need to be regularly reading Scripture.

This is why this book is constantly referring to Scripture, and Bible reading should be part of our regular prayer life, because it is God's chief communication with us. It is through it that we know of Jesus' life, death and resurrection. It is through it that we know all that led up to those events, and why the world is as it is. The Holy Spirit can bring the Bible to life for us, and speak to us personally through it. We should always ask for the help of the Holy Spirit as we read Scripture, as spiritual things can only be rightly understood as he enlightens our spiritual understanding.

God also speaks to us through people and through situations. Not everything that is said to us is from God, and not everything in our lives is necessarily according to the will of God. But when we are praying faithfully we may find that someone will say something that speaks to us at a deep level that gives us God's peace, or that something will happen that confirms what God seems to have been saying to us in our prayer time.

God can also speak to us through prophetic words or pictures. The Bible is full of both words and pictures through which God spoke, and he still does speak today. The word 'prophecy' means to 'show forth', not necessarily to tell the future, and prophecy often shows us the situation as God sees it. If a picture comes to mind, it is important to pray about it, and ask God the Holy Spirit to show you what it means, because a great deal depends on the interpretation. It is possible to have a genuine communication from God, but misunderstand or misinterpret it. When we receive words or a picture, it is always a vexed question as to whether it is from God or not. Time will tell, but God's own picture of a situation will help us to pray his will into being, so this kind of prophetic ministry often goes hand in hand with the ministry of intercession.

In the Bible we find pictures given by God to show forth a situation, followed by interpretation of the pictures. For example,

> The hand of the Lord was upon me, and he brought me out by the Spirit of the Lord and set me in the middle of a valley; it was full of bones. He led me to and fro among them, and I saw a great many bones on the floor of the valley, bones that were very dry. He asked me, 'Son of man, can these bones live?'
>
> I said, 'O Sovereign Lord, you alone know.'
>
> Then he said to me, 'Prophesy to these bones and say to them, "Dry bones, hear the word of the Lord! This is what the Sovereign Lord says to these bones: I will make breath enter you, and you

will come to life. I will attach tendons to you and make flesh come upon you and cover you with skin; I will put breath in you and you will come to life. Then you will know that I am the Lord." '

So I prophesied as I was commanded. And as I was prophesying, there was a noise, a rattling sound, and the bones came together, bone to bone. I looked, and tendons and flesh appeared on them and skin covered them, but there was no breath in them.

Then he said to me, 'Prophesy to the breath; prophesy, son of man, and say to it, "This is what the Sovereign Lord says: Come from the four winds, O breath, and breathe into these slain, that they may live." ' So I prophesied as he commanded me, and breath entered them; they came to life and stood up on their feet – a vast army.

Then he said to me: 'Son of man, these bones are the whole house of Israel. They say, "Our bones are dried up and our hope is gone; we are cut off." Therefore prophesy and say to them: "This is what the Sovereign Lord says: O my people, I am going to open your graves and bring you up from them; I will bring you back to the land of Israel. Then you, my people, will know that I am the Lord, when I open your graves and bring you up from them. I will put my Spirit in you and you will live, and I will settle you in your own land. Then you will know that I the Lord have spoken, and I have done it, declares the Lord." ' (Ezekiel 37.1–14)

Most often God will speak to us at a deeper level than words, through a deep peace, or through his love and joy welling up in our heart, or through what happens in the rest of the day. Sometimes it is only as we look back that we realize that God has been speaking to us all the time, but we have not 'heard' him. Sometimes when we are most anxious for him to speak we meet with a deafening silence. God wants us to trust him, and he responds to our faith. He reveals himself to those who confide in him, but to his accusers he said nothing. So we must approach him in humility but with confidence, knowing that we are loved and cherished. When we wait on him, he is able to enter our lives and show us his will for them, but our own wishes can mislead us, so we need the help of other Christians who also listen to God to find the way forward with us.

It is important to realize that there are times in our prayer life when God does speak, and other times when he is totally silent. The silent times are like a desert experience when we appear to be stumbling along entirely alone. These are times of testing and pruning, but we should not give up. God has not left us, but appears to have withdrawn to a distance. These times of pruning will lead to new growth if we persevere through them. The desert experience is common to all who are serious in prayer, and we should not be discouraged, but look forward to the time when our intimacy with God is renewed. There are times like this in the Old Testament when 'there was no word from the Lord in those days', but again God raised up a new people with whom he did communicate and to whom he revealed himself.

Today is a time when God is speaking to many Christians; the difficulty is what it has always been – to distinguish between false and true prophecy, and to distinguish between our own wishes and God speaking to us. However, when his authority was being questioned, Jesus said, 'My sheep listen to my voice, I know them, and they follow me.'[1] Any true communication from God will help us to love and serve him better, and will help us to follow Jesus more faithfully. That is the touchstone that we need to judge by, as we listen for what God may have to say to us. If we are seriously wanting to follow Jesus, we will recognize his voice and respond to him, as Bishop Hugh Montefiore did right at the beginning of his Christian life.

Exercises

- Read John 10:22–30 and meditate on it. Do you have the personal relationship with Jesus that he speaks of in verses 27 and 28? If not, ask him to make you his own. If you already have a relationship with Jesus, is it growing, deepening, developing? Thank and praise him for this relationship and ask him to lead you on.
- Survey your present life and circumstances. What do you think that God is saying to you through them?
- Sometimes God speaks to us through his creation. Take a prayer walk through a park, in the countryside or by the sea, and listen to the sights and sounds of his creation. Or take something God has made – a flower or plant or seashell – and ask God to speak to you through it or about it.
- Sometimes God speaks to us in the form of prophecy. Read Ezekiel 37 and see how God spoke to Ezekiel about Israel through a picture, and then interpreted the picture for him so that he understood what it meant.

A Prayer for God's Guidance

Lord Jesus,
You have called us to follow you.
Help us to hear your voice,
To respond to your call,
To follow you,
And to do your will,
Day by day.

Amen.

9

LEARNING TO BE ONESELF

Many people think that in order to speak to God, they have got to put on special language, or a special voice, or a special persona that will somehow impress him. But God is not interested in the masks we put on. The person he loves, and wishes to converse with, is the real you, the true self that we seldom are in ordinary social activity. We have simply to be ourselves; but that is not as simple as it appears. We are so used to living behind a mask that we have forgotten who our real self is, and it rarely shows itself, except in moments of anger, or grief, or love, when we break through the shell behind which we live most of the time.

Most children up to about the age of six or seven are able to be their real selves; that is what is so refreshing about them. But as they grow up, in self-defence against an unkind world, and in order to please adults they retreat behind a shell which protects them socially, but which inhibits them from developing their real potential. As the building of these defences is not the work of a day, it will take you and the Holy Spirit some time to dismantle what has taken you years to perfect. The defences are crippling your development, and need to come down to enable you to be your real self once more. Someone said to me, 'It has taken me most of my lifetime to discover who I really am, and to have the courage to be that.'

A friend who restores frescoes found that behind a rather ordinary medieval painting on the wall of a chapel in Winchester Cathedral was a stunning picture of Christ, probably painted by the master painter at the court of Henry III in the thirteenth century. Through a miracle of modern technology, she was able to remove the top painting intact and put it somewhere else, and reveal the hidden masterpiece underneath, fresh as it was on the day it was painted. This is the kind of work that you and the Holy Spirit together must embark on if you are to develop your relationship with God. The work of your prayer life is not just about discovering more of God; it is a work of discovering who you really are – the person that God made in his image, and to whom he wishes to be united in love.

If we understand more of our true personality, it will help us to know how to pray. An aid to discovering more about ourselves has been developed called the Myers–Briggs Typology Indicator, which assesses our personality according to preferences that were noted by Jung in his work as a psychologist.

For example, where do I get emotional energy from? How do I recharge my batteries? If I am an extrovert, I will find my energy from the outer world of people and external activity. If I am an introvert, I will recharge my batteries by withdrawing into silence and solitude. The application of this to prayer is obvious. The introvert will find it easy to withdraw to have a quiet time with God. The extrovert will look to find God in other people and in external activity. This does not mean that an extrovert cannot learn to pray silently in a quiet time, or that an introvert cannot find God in external activity or other people, but that it will require more effort.

If you wish to find out more about the Myers–Briggs Typology Indicator, I recommend that you read the excellent book, *Pray Your Way: Your Personality and God* by Bruce Duncan, published by Darton, Longman and Todd. Even better, go on a Myers–Briggs Basic Workshop, on which your personality type will be tested and explained. After doing the basic workshop, there are additional workshops on spirituality and prayer, and the shadow side of personality. The shadow side is not necessarily our faults or shortcomings. In Jungian terms it is that side of ourselves that lies hidden and neglected because we have turned in the opposite direction. Jung believed that it was the job of the second half of our lives to work on the shadow side which had been neglected in the first half. Particulars of Myers–Briggs workshops may be found in *Vision* magazine, available from the National Retreat Association, The Central Hall, 256 Bermondsey Street, London SE1 3UJ; telephone 0171 357 7736.

Remember when you pray that you are meeting your Maker, who knows all about you. It is useless to pretend or put on masks in front of him. Remember also that he loves you as you are. Talk to him simply and from your heart; not disguising your anger, your boredom, your irritation or whatever. Let him, like the fresco-restorer, lift off the outer covering, and leave you vulnerable in front of him, but yourself.

O Lord, you have searched me and you know me,
You know when I sit and when I rise;
you perceive my thoughts from afar
You discern my going out and my lying down;
you are familiar with all my ways.
Before a word is on my tongue
you know it completely, O Lord.

You hem me in, behind and before;
you have laid your hand upon me.
Such knowledge is too wonderful for me,
too lofty for me to attain. . . .

Search me, O God, and know my heart,
test me and know my anxious thoughts.
See if there is any offensive way in me,
and lead me in the way everlasting.
(Psalm 139)

Exercises

- Meditate on Psalm 139, and out of it make your prayer to God.
- Read the book, *Pray Your Way*, and make notes on what helps you most.
- Go to a Myers–Briggs Basic Workshop and learn all you can about your own personality type.
- Ask God to help you to be your real self and to heal you of all that prevents your healthy development. Make a self-portrait and show it to someone who knows you well. How well do you in fact know yourself? Pray for self-knowledge and the courage to be yourself.

Part 3
Different Kinds of Prayer

10

PETITION

> Then [Jesus] said to them, 'Suppose one of you has a friend, and he goes to him at midnight and says, "Friend, lend me three loaves of bread, because a friend of mine on a journey has come to me, and I have nothing to set before him."
>
> 'Then the one inside answers, "Don't bother me. The door is already locked, and my children are with me in bed. I can't get up and give you anything." I tell you, though he will not get up and give him the bread because he is his friend, yet because of the man's boldness he will get up and give him as much as he needs.
>
> 'So I say to you: Ask and it will be given to you, seek and you will find; knock and the door will be opened to you. For everyone who asks receives; he who seeks finds, and to him who knocks, the door will be opened.
>
> 'Which of you fathers, if your son asks for a fish, will give him a snake instead? Or if he asks for an egg, will give him a scorpion? If you then, though you are evil, know how to give good gifts to your children, how much more will your Father in heaven give the Holy Spirit to those who ask him!' (Luke 11.5–13)

When the disciples asked Jesus to teach them to pray, he gave them the Lord's Prayer as a model and guide, and then taught them about the prayer of petition. The prayer of petition is one in which we ask God for something that is on our heart – not to be confused with the prayer of intercession, when we pray on behalf of others – and listen to God so that we can try to discern what is on his heart.

Jesus starts with the parable of the man who comes to his friend at midnight, asking for food to give a friend who has visited him, and to whom custom demanded that he should give hospitality. To begin with he gets a dusty answer: the friend is in bed, and his children with him; he doesn't want to disturb them by getting up. But because of the boldness and persistence of the man, the neighbour gets up and gives him what he wants. It is the boldness and the persistence of the man that Jesus wants us to emulate. Jesus tells another parable with the same theme:

> Then Jesus told his disciples a parable to show them that they should always pray and not give up. He said: 'In a certain town there was a judge who neither feared God nor cared about men. And there was a widow in that town who kept coming to him with the plea, "Grant me justice against my adversary."
>
> 'For some time he refused. But finally he said to himself, "Even though I don't fear God or care about men, yet because this widow keeps bothering me, I will see that she gets justice, so that she won't eventually wear me out with her coming!" '
>
> And the Lord said, 'Listen to what the unjust judge says.'
>
> (Luke 18.1–6)

Here we have the same idea: the unjust judge cannot at first be bothered with the widow, who would not have had any money to encourage him to take up her cause. But because she keeps on bothering him, he gives way for a quiet life and sees that she gets justice. How much more, says Jesus, will God hear the prayers of his people who cry out to him day and night? Again, boldness and persistence are what Jesus is urging us to have when we come to God in the prayer of petition. Also faith, as the last sentence implies. We need to trust God that he will answer our prayers. James, the brother of Jesus, tells us:

> If any of you lacks wisdom, he should ask God, who gives generously to all without finding fault, and it will be given to him. But when he asks, he must believe and not doubt, because he who doubts is like a wave of the sea, blown and tossed by the wind. That man should not think he will receive anything from the Lord; he is a double-minded man, unstable in all he does.
>
> (James 1.5–8)

So when we pray the prayer of petition we must have boldness, persistence and faith – a real confidence that God can and will give us what we ask. We should then look for our prayer to be answered. We should have in mind that God always answers prayer, but not always in the way that we expect. His thoughts are higher than our thoughts, and he may answer our prayer in a more appropriate way than it was formulated. Also his timescale is different from ours. The answer may not come straightaway and we may have to wait and watch and go on praying. This is when persistence is needed.

We need to remember that sentence in the Lord's Prayer: 'Forgive us our sins as we forgive those who sin against us.' In order to pray to God we need to come repentant of our own sins, and forgiving of others; otherwise our prayers will not be heard. So first clear with God anything that stands between you and him, and ask for forgiveness for Jesus Christ's sake, and make an act of forgiveness towards anyone who has sinned against you, so that nothing may impede your prayer of petition.

Then remember Jesus' wonderful words of encouragement: 'Ask and it will be given to you; seek and you will find; knock and the door will be opened to you.'[1] Be encouraged, and persevere in prayer. And remember that the good gift, the best gift that God can give us in prayer is that of the Holy Spirit. He is the best answer to all our prayers. In Jesus' time, the Holy Spirit would have been thought of as a special gift for special people. It is only since Pentecost that he has been seen as a gift for those who believe Jesus to be the Son of God, and who follow him. Even though we have been baptized and given the Holy Spirit, we need to continue to ask for him. We also need to ask the Holy Spirit for his gifts so that we can live according to the will of God. We need his wisdom, his guidance, his continual infilling, his gift of knowledge, and his power to do the work of God. So ask so that you can receive all the blessing that he has to give you and be filled with his love, his joy, his peace.

Exercises

- Meditate on the biblical passages in the text. If there is anything that particularly strikes you, or you find difficult to understand, bring it in prayer to God. End with this prayer:

  Come, Holy Spirit,
  Please help us to pray.
  Give us faith and trust that we are heard.
  Give us boldness and persistence in asking.
  We ask that our prayers be answered
  Through Jesus Christ our Lord
  To the glory of God the Father.
  Amen

- Ask the Holy Spirit for a gift of knowledge to know whether there is anything that stands in the way of your prayers being heard – any lack of forgiveness or repentance on your part. If anything comes to mind, bring it to God and ask for forgiveness for Jesus' sake, and ask to be made willing to forgive all who sin against you. Then make a list of your real needs – spiritual and material – and bring them to the Father through the Son.

The Wind

The wind tugs at the house
And hums in the chimney.
The trees sway like dancers
And the bushes nod their heads.
The loft lids rattle.
My cat cowers and runs for shelter
Into the still warm house
Which stands like a lighthouse
As the westerly runs in from the sea
Across the valley
To hit the house full on.

So come, Holy Spirit,
Blow on me like the westerly wind.
Blow away the rubbish,
The junk ideas,
The self-indulgence.
Brace me, so that I can live
As God intends.
Set me free to live
The destiny God has for me,
So much greater
Than anything I can think of.
Blow away all that hinders
The work of God in me.

Give me your gifts,
So that I may give
Your life to others.
Give me your fruits,
So that I may glorify
The God who gives them,
And live your life
Rather than my own.
So may it be so, Holy Spirit.

Wind of God, come blow on me.
Accomplish the work of God in me
And make me new.

Amen

11

INTERCESSION

To 'intercede' literally means to 'ask on behalf of others'. It means to stand between God and the people for whom we pray, identifying completely with both. To pray on behalf of others we need to be right with God. Just as we did with the prayer of petition, we need to check with God whether there is anything standing between us and God before we pray. We need to come before God repentant of our sin and forgiving of other people's sins if our prayers are to be heard. Through Christ we can be right with God, and 'The prayer of a righteous man is powerful and effective.'[1]

James 5.13–20 is worth looking at in greater detail. He says:

> Is any one of you in trouble? He should pray. Is anyone happy? Let him sing songs of praise. Is any one of you sick? He should call the elders of the church to pray over him and anoint him with oil in the name of the Lord. And the prayer offered in faith will make the sick person well; the Lord will raise him up. If he has sinned, he will be forgiven. Therefore confess your sins to each other and pray for each other so that you may be healed. The prayer of a righteous man is powerful and effective.
>
> Elijah was a man just like us. He prayed earnestly that it would not rain, and it did not rain on the land for three and a half years. Again he prayed, and the heavens gave rain, and the earth produced its crops.
>
> My brothers, if one of you should wander from the truth and someone should bring him back, remember this: Whoever turns a sinner from the error of his way will save him from death and cover a multitude of sins.

We are to pray for those in trouble and for those who are sick; confess our sins and pray for each other to be forgiven; pray for sinners to be brought back to the truth. One of the most encouraging things about the Church today is the rediscovery of the healing ministry. James supposes that this healing ministry should be part of the regular life of the Church, and that this will be done on behalf of the Church by the elders, the leaders of the congregation.

Jesus tells us very specifically that we should pray for our enemies and those who persecute us, which is much more difficult than praying for the sick or those in trouble who naturally engage our sympathy. Yet we who are offended by the behaviour of others, are in the best position to pray for them. Jesus tells us:

> You have heard that it was said, 'Love your neighbour and hate your enemy.' But I tell you: Love your enemies and pray for those who persecute you, that you may be sons of your Father in heaven. He causes his sun to rise on the evil and the good, and sends rain on the righteous and the unrighteous. If you love those who love you, what reward will you get? Are not even the tax collectors doing that? And if you greet only your brothers, what are you doing more than others? Do not even pagans do that? Be perfect, therefore, as your heavenly Father is perfect.
>
> (Matthew 5.43–8)

As the ones who are sinned against, we have the power to release those who have offended against us by forgiving them. This is easier said than done. It is human to sin, but divine to forgive. We don't need necessarily to have the right feelings, except to be willing to forgive as we ourselves have been forgiven. So we must pray for our enemies, and it is a sign of God's life indwelling in us and guiding us when we are able to pray for those whom we find difficult. It is a real test of our vocation as Christians.

We also need to pray for the community within which we are set: our family, our church, our town or village, and our nation. But how are we to pray? There is no need to tell God what to do, he knows much better than we do what is needed. Neither should we approach God with a shopping list on behalf of others. We should remember who it is we are praying to – the Maker of all things – and listen to what he has to say on the subject too. He has his plans for the person or people we are praying for, and we need to chime in with that. So we must listen to God, and hear his point of view, as well as coming to him with our wishes for other people.

If we are not clear what we should pray for another person, we should pray that God's will be done in their lives, and that he will bless them with his love, his joy, and his peace. We need to lift the person up to God, repent on their behalf if they are going wrong, and remind God of the promises in his Word to forgive and love us for Christ's sake. All prayer should be an alignment of ourselves with the perfect purposes of God. When we pray for others, we need to align ourselves with his purpose for their lives, and be a bridge, a channel, through which God's will can be done by the power of prayer. We are spreading the kingdom, the place where God's kingly rule is established, when we undertake the prayer of intercession.

Exercises

- Meditate on James 5:13–20. Are you doing what James is asking us to do in this passage? If anything is lacking ask God to help you to respond by doing it. End with a time of intercession for those whose names come to your mind.
- Meditate on Matthew 5:43–8. If you have nobody who you can call an enemy, or who opposes you in any way, think of and pray for those whom you find it difficult to get on with. It may be that things in your church are not as you would like them to be, or there is someone in your family you find it hard to relate to. Ask for forgiveness for what you perceive to be wrong, and pray for God's will to be done in your church, or in your family.
- There are several prayer initiatives which call on Christians to pray for Britain. One of them, Crosswinds,[2] calls on churches to give a week a year to prayer for the Church and for the nation. Their prayer is based on Nehemiah 1.5–11 where the prophet prays for the nation of Israel. Look at the passage and discern what it has to teach you about intercession. Then compare it with the Crosswinds prayer which is a Christian version of Nehemiah's prayer. Use the Crosswinds prayer to pray for the nation.

  Then I said: 'O Lord, God of heaven, the great and awesome God, who keeps his covenant of love with those who love him and obey his commands, let your ear be attentive and your eyes open to hear the prayer your servant is praying before you day and night for your servants, the people of Israel. I confess the sins we Israelites, including myself and my father's house, have committed against you. We have acted very wickedly towards you. We have not obeyed the commands, decrees and laws you gave your servant Moses.

  Remember the instruction you gave your servant Moses, saying, "If you are unfaithful, I will scatter you among the nations, but if you return to me and obey my commands, then even if your exiled people are at the farthest horizon, I will gather them from there and bring them to the place I have chosen as a dwelling for my Name."

'They are your servants and your people, whom you redeemed by your great strength and your mighty hand. O Lord, let your ear be attentive to the prayer of . . . your servants who delight in revering your name. Give your servant success today by granting him favour in the presence of this man.' (Nehemiah 1.5–11)

The Crosswinds Prayer for Britain

Lord God of heaven, you are great and we stand in awe of you. You faithfully keep your new covenant with those people who trust in you and in Jesus Christ, whom you have sent. Look down on us, Lord, and hear our prayers as we pray for your Church here in this nation. We confess that we, your people, have sinned. We and all the people of this nation have gone away from you and your gospel, the Good News about Jesus Christ.

Remember now what you have done in him and not what we deserve. For his sake renew and restore your people, rebuild your Church and win this nation for Christ and his gospel once again.

We ask this in his name and for your honour and glory.

Amen

12

PRAISE

To 'praise', according to the *Oxford Dictionary*, is to 'express warm approbation of, to commend the merits of a person or thing, to glorify, to extol the attributes of a person or thing'. We praise God because he is praiseworthy, not because he is sitting there, so to speak, waiting for us to praise him. 'Great is the Lord and most worthy of praise' says Psalm 145.3. All the last six psalms in the book of Psalms are songs of praise, but Psalm 145 is the most comprehensive. It is attributed to David, and tells us why God is worthy of our praise. It shows us why praise is such an important element of worship. To worship God is to give him his worth, to adore him, and Psalm 145 gives God his worth and praises him for it.

I will exalt you, my God the King;
    I will praise your name for ever and ever.
Every day I will praise you
    and extol your name for ever and ever.

Great is the Lord and most worthy of praise;
    his greatness no-one can fathom.
One generation will commend your works to another;
    they will tell of your mighty acts.
They will speak of the glorious splendour of your majesty,
    and I will meditate on your wonderful works.
They will tell of the power of your awesome works,
    and I will proclaim your great deeds.
They will celebrate your abundant goodness
    and joyfully sing of your righteousness.

The Lord is gracious and compassionate,
    slow to anger and rich in love.
The Lord is good to all;
    he has compassion on all he has made.
All you have made will praise you, O Lord;
    your saints will extol you.

They will tell of the glory of your kingdom
  and speak of your might,
so that all men may know of your mighty acts
  and the glorious splendour of your kingdom.
Your kingdom is an everlasting kingdom,
  and your dominion endures through all generations.

The Lord is faithful to all his promises
  and loving towards all he has made.
The Lord upholds all those who fall
  and lifts up all who are bowed down.
The eyes of all look to you,
  and you give them their food at the proper time.
You open your hand
  and satisfy the desires of every living thing.

The Lord is righteous in all his ways
  and loving towards all he has made.
The Lord is near to all who call on him,
  to all who call on him in truth.
He fulfils the desires of those who fear him;
  he hears their cry and saves them.
The Lord watches over all who love him,
  but all the wicked he will destroy.

My mouth will speak in praise of the Lord.
Let every creature praise his holy name
  for ever and ever.

(Psalm 145)

Psalm 145 shows us why praise is a fitting reaction to the goodness and the greatness of God. The Hebrew name for the book of Psalms is '*Tehillim*', which means praises. The Psalms are the greatest collection of prayers and songs of praise that exists, and we can help ourselves to pray by including one of them in our daily prayer time. There is a psalm for every mood and every occasion, but Psalm 145 is the outstanding psalm of praise, which we can study to understand the true nature of praise. We praise God because of what he is – loving and compassionate towards everything and everyone he has made – and because of what he has done. What he has done for all of us as individuals is recorded in the Bible. He has given his Son for us on the cross, the most precious gift of all. What he has done additionally for us is known only to us, but we must remember to thank and praise him for all his gifts.

Praise is a sign that the Holy Spirit has the freedom to work within us and turn us to God. There are naturally times when we feel less like praising God because of bereavement or other distress. But it is important that we should continue to offer God a sacrifice of praise, because he is still great and wonderful, whatever we may feel like at the time. We praise him because he deserves our praise, not because of our feelings. However, praise of God has the power to lift us up, no matter what is happening to us. As we bless and praise God, and tell him we love him, he blesses us and lifts us up. The great hymn of praise, 'All creatures of our God and King', is based on a poem which was written by St Francis of Assisi when he lay sick and dying. No trace of his circumstances are within it except the beautiful verse on death (verse 6) which is often left out. All we are conscious of is the great joy that fills it, the Franciscan joy in the goodness and greatness of God, and which cries out to the whole of creation to join him in praise to God.

All creatures of our God and King

1 All creatures of our God and King,
lift up your voice and with us sing:
Alleluia, alleluia!
Thou burning sun with golden beam,
thou silver moon with softer gleam;
O praise him, O praise him,
Alleluia, alleluia, alleluia!

2 Thou rushing wind that art so strong,
Ye clouds that sail in heaven along,
O praise him, alleluia!
Thou rising morn, in praise rejoice,
Ye lights of evening, find a voice;
O praise him, etc.

3 Thou flowing water, pure and clear,
Make music for thy Lord to hear,
Alleluia, alleluia!
Thou fire so masterful and bright,
That givest man both warmth and light.
O praise him, etc.

4 Dear mother earth, who day by day
Unfoldest blessings on our way,
O praise him, alleluia!
The flowers and fruits that in thee grow,
Let them his glory also show;
O praise him, etc.

5 And all ye men of tender heart,
Forgiving others, take your part,
O sing ye alleluia!
Ye who long pain and sorrow bear,
Praise God and on him cast your care;
O praise him, etc.

6 And thou, most kind and gentle death,
Waiting to hush our latest breath,
O praise him, alleluia!
Thou leadest home the child of God,
And Christ our Lord the way hath trod;
O praise him, etc.

7 Let all things their Creator bless,
And worship him in humbleness;
O praise him, alleluia!
Praise, praise the Father, praise the Son,
And praise the Spirit, Three in One;
O praise him, etc.

William Henry Draper (1855–1933)
based on Francis of Assisi (1182–1226)

Exercises

- Make a list of all the attributes of God that you can think of that deserve our praise, what he is, and what he has done. Praise God using Psalm 145.
- Use the hymn 'All creatures of our God and King' to help you to meditate on God as Creator. Finish by saying the hymn as a prayer.
- Make a list of all the things that God has done for you personally that you can remember. Write a prayer of praise to him for what he has done.

13

SAYING 'SORRY'

Praying is not an escape from reality, as some people think. It is rather a facing of reality in the light of God's truth, and he is the reality of all that is. As we come closer to God, we begin to see more of God's reality, but also the reality of ourselves, and both are humbling. We begin to be stripped of our fantasies about God and about ourselves, and to see things as they really are. Compared with other people, we may seem to be all right. Compared with God – his holiness, his goodness, his great love and compassion – we fall so short that we begin to realize, perhaps for the first time, what sinners we are. In fact, the closer we come to God, the worse we feel. The holiest of saints are the ones who are most conscious of their errors. It is not that we are getting worse but that we are becoming more aware, in the light of God, of just how wrong we are in many areas. The Holy Spirit convicts us of sin, and we know that we need God's forgiveness.

This is where the gospel comes in to help and save us. Jesus came into Galilee at the start of his ministry preaching the good news of the forgiveness of sins. On the cross he won that forgiveness for us. He has bridged the gulf that exists between a holy God and a sinful people, and has made it possible to win God's acceptance and forgiveness. All that is asked of us is to repent and believe the good news. To repent is to say 'Sorry' and to turn away from our sins to live as God has commanded us to: to love him and to love our neighbour. To believe the good news is to believe what God has done for us through Jesus Christ on the cross, and accept his love and forgiveness into our lives.

So we need to pray the prayer of contrition, that is to say 'Sorry' for those things we are conscious of that are wrong in our lives, and also those things which are still hidden from us. 'Human beings', says T. S. Eliot through the women of Canterbury in *Murder in the Cathedral*, 'cannot bear very much reality'. The Holy Spirit will only show us as much as we can bear about ourselves; there is much lurking in the unconscious still waiting to be dealt with.

Being sorry for our sins is only the first step, leading us to a real change of mind and heart. A woman once said in a PCC meeting,

'Don't ask me to change. I don't want to change. I want the church to be a comfort to me in my old age, not to ask me to change.' But the Christian life is all about change; it is about '*metanoia*', a Greek word we find in the Bible which means 'a change of mind and heart'. If we are really sorry for our sins, we will want to change, and the grace of the Holy Spirit will enable us to do what we cannot do by ourselves: to be changed, over a lifetime, into the likeness of Christ.

So repentance, or thinking again, is a growth point, and as Mother Basilea Schlink pointed out in her book, *Repentance: The Joy-filled Life*, it is a recipe for a happy life. It may be painful and hard at the time, but it is the way to the joy of the gospel, knowing that we are accepted, loved and forgiven in Christ, in spite of our faults, and made right with God. It is a good practice to make a regular self-examination, asking the Holy Spirit to pinpoint anything that is wrong so that it can be dealt with. True contrition only comes as the result of the Holy Spirit showing us what is wrong, and showing us something of the greatness and glory of God. But whatever you do, do not let a consciousness of sin cast you down to the point where you fail to receive the wonderful love and forgiveness of God which is promised to all who believe in him, and Jesus Christ whom he has sent. Your forgiveness has already been won for you on the cross. Receive it with joy and thanksgiving and ask for the grace to receive it so that you are able to change. Remember that the important thing when you fall down is not to sit on the ground but to get up again. Jesus extends his hand to lift you up and get you going again. If you find that there is something that haunts you and will not go away, ask a Christian whom you trust for help and ministry.

The only thing we have to fear is complacency. Jesus had very little to say to those who thought they were all right, but a great deal of time and love and compassion for those who knew they were sinners. He told this story to illustrate the point.

> To some who were confident of their own righteousness and looked down on everybody else, Jesus told this parable: 'Two men went up to the temple to pray, one a Pharisee and the other a tax collector. The Pharisee stood up and prayed about himself: "God, I thank you that I am not like other men – robbers, evil-doers, adulterers – or even like this tax collector. I fast twice a week and give a tenth of all I get."
>
> 'But the tax collector stood at a distance. He would not even

look up to heaven, but beat his breast and said, "God, have mercy on me, a sinner."

'I tell you that this man, rather than the other, went home justified before God. For everyone who exalts himself will be humbled, and he who humbles himself will be exalted.' (Luke 18.9–14)

Other Bible passages you could look up are: John 1.29; Psalm 51; John 8.1–11; 1 John 1.5–10; 2.1–2; Psalm 145.8–9.

Exercises

- Use one or some of the Bible passages given above as a meditation and make up your own prayer based on it.
- Ask the Holy Spirit to help you make a self-examination, using Luke 10.25–37 as a yardstick. Finish with your own prayer of contrition to God.
- Ask the Holy Spirit to help you make a self-examination, using Exodus 20.1–17 as a yardstick. Finish with your own prayer of contrition to God.
- Here is a collect from the Alternative Service Book which is a prayer for pardon and peace. Say it for yourself and for your own community.

Merciful Lord,
grant to your faithful people pardon and peace:
that we may be cleansed from all our sins
and serve you with a quiet mind;
through Jesus Christ our Lord.

Love

Love bade me welcome; yet my soul drew back,
    Guilty of dust and sin.
But quick-ey'd Love, observing me grow slack
    From my first entrance in,
Drew nearer to me, sweetly questioning,
    If I lack'd anything.
A guest, I answered, worthy to be here:
    Love said, You shall be he.
I, the unkind, ungrateful? Ah my dear,
    I cannot look on thee.
Love took my hand, and smiling did reply,
    Who made the eyes but I?
Truth, Lord, but I have marr'd them: let my shame
    Go where it doth deserve.
And know you not, says Love, who bore the blame?
    My dear, then I will serve.
You must sit down, says Love, and taste my meat:
    So I did sit and eat.

George Herbert (1593–1633)

14

THANKSGIVING

> Be joyful always; pray continually; give thanks in all circumstances, for this is God's will for you in Christ Jesus.
> (1 Thessalonians 5.16–18)

> Rejoice in the Lord always. I will say it again: Rejoice! Let your gentleness be evident to all. The Lord is near. Do not be anxious about anything, but in everything, by prayer and petition, with thanksgiving, present your requests to God. And the peace of God, which transcends all understanding, will guard your hearts and your minds in Christ Jesus. (Philippians 4.4–7)

One of the first lessons in etiquette we are taught as children is to say 'Thank you'. A little girl who was making her first prayer to God was told to ask for anything she wanted, and so she asked God for a bracelet. Her mother heard the prayer and bought her a bracelet. She was delighted with it, but had to be reminded to say thank you to her mother and to God for it. When we ask God for anything we need to look for the answer to our prayer, even if it is not what we expected, and then to thank God for it.

But the Bible readings at the head of this page tell us to do more than that. We are to have joyful, thankful hearts; not just when we are given what we want, but 'in all circumstances'. And in Philippians we read why we are to rejoice in the Lord always. God is constant. He is always loving, compassionate, kind and gracious whatever our circumstances are, so we can always rejoice in him and what he is, and what he has done.

We are told not to be anxious about anything, but in everything to present our requests to God *with thanksgiving*. We need to be continually thanking God for all his goodness to us. 'Count your blessings one by one', the old song goes, and we need to remember all the ways in which God has blessed us. We can so easily forget, like the little girl. Israel remembered what God had done for her in psalms like Psalm 107 and Psalm 136, and the Church remembers what

Christ has done for us continually in the Eucharist. The very word 'Eucharist' means 'thanksgiving'.

A grateful heart is a happy and peaceful one. If we remember our blessings and thank God for them we will have his joy and his peace, whatever our circumstances. So let your prayers have thanksgiving as a continual theme, and let your heart be grateful to God for all his gifts to us, but particularly for his gift of himself, his Son, and his Holy Spirit to us, now, and for evermore.

Exercises

- Make a list of the blessings that you can think of to thank God for. Make a prayer of thanksgiving in your own words.
- Meditate on the biblical texts at the beginning of this section, and end with the General Thanksgiving.

Almighty God, Father of all mercies,
we your unworthy servants do give you most humble and hearty thanks
for all your goodness and loving kindness
to us and to all people.
We bless you for our creation, preservation, and all the blessings of this life;
but above all for your immeasurable love
in the redemption of the world by our Lord Jesus Christ,
for the means of grace, and for the hope of glory.
And give us, we pray, such a sense of all your mercies
that our hearts may be unfeignedly thankful,
and that we show forth your praise,
not only with our lips but in our lives,
by giving up ourselves to your service,
and by walking before you in holiness and righteousness all our days;
through Jesus Christ our Lord,
to whom, with you and the Holy Spirit,
be all honour and glory,
for ever and ever. Amen

The Alternative Service Book 1980

15

PRAYER OF THE HEART

It has been said that the longest journey that we have to make is that from the head to the heart. Most of us have been taught to distrust or guard our heart – our intuitive, feeling side – and to sieve everything through the intellect. But if we look at the Bible, even if we only look up a fraction of the more than two hundred references to the word 'heart', it is clear that the biblical view is that we chiefly respond or otherwise to God in our heart, and that the word 'heart' covers the will as well as the emotions, the hidden unconscious mind as well as the feeling part of us; our understanding, rather than our intellect.

For example, in Proverbs we are told:

My son, if you accept my words
and store up my commands within you,
turning your ear to wisdom
and applying your heart to understanding . . .
Then you will understand what is right and just
and fair – every good path.
For wisdom will enter your heart,
and knowledge will be pleasant to your soul.
(Proverbs 2.1, 2, 9, 10)

Thus spiritual understanding is a matter of the heart rather than just the mind. The heart is right at the very centre of our being, and it is to the heart that God's divine gift of wisdom is given. It is a matter of feeling, not just of intellectual satisfaction. The knowledge that God gives will be pleasant to the soul. In chapter 3 of Proverbs we are told:

Keep my commands in your heart,
Let love and faithfulness never leave you . . .
write them on the tablet of your heart.
Trust in the Lord with all your heart
and lean not on your own understanding;
in all your ways acknowledge him,
and he will make your paths straight.
(Proverbs 3.1, 3, 5, 6)

In other words, our righteousness depends on how our heart is disposed. We are to keep the Lord's commands in our heart, even to write them on the tablet of our heart. We are to trust the Lord with *all* our heart, and then he will make our path straight, and we will be acceptable to him.

The opposite of this is to be hard-hearted. We are told in Exodus 4.21 that God will harden Pharaoh's heart so that he will not let the people of Israel go. Jesus says that those who do not hear his words are unable to see and hear because their hearts are hardened.[1] And 'out of the unclean heart come evil thoughts', says Jesus, 'murder, adultery, sexual immorality, theft, false testimony, slander'.[2] But Jesus also says, 'Blessed are the pure in heart, for they will see God.'[3]

So a pure heart is vital in our relationship with God, but what do we mean by the 'heart' in this context, and what do we mean by 'prayer of the heart'?

As I understand it, the heart is right at the centre of our being, and when we feel strongly our heart feels moved. It is also the centre of our will, where our most important decisions are made or influenced. It is the seat of our emotions, and we guard our heart so that we are not swept away by exterior or interior forces. But, the Bible says, if it is clean, and right with God, our heart will lead us in the right direction; and the most powerful prayers we can say or offer come welling up from the heart, which encompasses all the deepest and hidden parts of our personality.

We cannot comprehend God with the intellect, because he is greater than our thoughts or our imagination. But we can know God in our heart because he is love and the heart knows what love is, and responds with love. So the prayer of the heart is a wordless prayer of love and adoration, a prayer of the affections or feelings, and is sometimes called 'affective prayer'.

Many of the modern choruses are love songs to Jesus or the Father which enable this transaction of love to take place. Their repetitive mantra-like words help us to focus on the Lord without being too verbally demanding. A 'mantra' is a word or phrase which keeps our mind from wandering off and focuses us on God while we love and adore him in our hearts. Feelings are important here, and music has the power to touch our hearts and turn them towards God, which we may find difficult to do 'from cold' as it were. This is not a prayer we can practise; we may only open ourselves to it, and allow our hearts to move when it comes. It is not the be-all and end-all of prayer. We often don't have the right feelings when we come before God and that is all right, but when it happens we need to rejoice that the deepest part of our being has come awake at his touch. We will not need words necessarily to pray this prayer – only such words as lovers use, as we offer God our love, our adoration, and our reverence at his holiness – for this prayer of the heart is pleasing to his heart.

Exercises

- The Psalms are full of prayers about the heart – here are a few short prayers taken from different psalms.

May the words of my mouth
and the meditation of my heart
be pleasing in your sight,
O Lord, my Rock and my Redeemer.
(Psalm 19.14)

Create in me a pure heart, O God,
and renew a steadfast spirit within me.
Do not cast me from your presence
or take your Holy Spirit from me.
Restore to me the joy of your salvation
and grant me a willing spirit, to sustain me.
(Psalm 51.10–12)

Teach me your way, O Lord,
and I will walk in your truth;
give me an undivided heart,
that I may fear your name.
I will praise you, O Lord my God, with all my heart;
I will glorify your name for ever.
(Psalm 86.11, 12)

- Here are one or two of the love songs that we sing nowadays – you may know others that are suitable to use. The first one can be sung in the singular or the plural.

Father, we/I adore you,
Lay our/my lives/life before you,
How we/I love you.
Jesus, we/I adore you, etc.
Spirit, we/I adore you, etc.
(Terry Coelho, © 1972 Maranatha!/Word Music)

I love you, Lord, and I lift my voice
To worship you, O my soul rejoice.
Take joy, my king, in what you hear,
May it be a sweet, sweet sound in your ear.
(Laurie Klein, © 1978 Maranatha!/Word Music)

I just want to praise you,
Lift my hands and say: 'I love you.'
You are everything to me
And I exalt your holy name on high.
(Arthur Tannous, copyright © 1984
Acts Music/Kingsway's Thankyou Music,
PO Box 75, Eastbourne, E. Sussex, BN23 6NT, UK.
Used by kind permission of Kingsway's Thankyou Music.)

Derby Day

Everything is fresh and green and lush
After the summer rain.
Now the summer sun
Brings heat to this glorious morning.
The may is thick with blossom,
The horse chestnuts studded with candles.
The first roses unfold,
And the peonies hang heavy
With their rich full flowers.
Nature has reached a sumptuous peak
As the fresh new life bursts into bloom
And summer is really here.
The back door is open to the fragrant air,
And the cool shade of the cottage is pleasant.
My cat Sheba wanders in and out
Enjoying the sunshine,
Keeping an eye on her garden,
Inspecting every nook and cranny.
On the main road the holidaymakers
Hurry down to Devon and Cornwall,
Oblivious of the beauties on either side,
Leaving us in peace in this tranquil backwater.
For heaven is now and here
To be found by those who seek,
By those whose eyes are open,
And whose ears are tuned
To the sound of silence.
While the madding crowd
Rush blindly by,
Missing the moment.
Looking for pleasure
But losing the joy
Of the quiet disclosure
To the waiting heart.

16

CONTEMPLATION

The prayer of contemplation has been described as 'looking at God and loving him'. But it is also a prayer of receiving God's love and grace. 'Contemplation' is rather a blanket word which means different things to different people. There are schools of contemplation which have varying emphases, and it is a matter of finding which one suits your personality type.

The gift of contemplation, and it is a gift from God, usually manifests itself to begin with by a desire for stillness and quiet. The person just wants to be with God, aware of his presence, but without words. Very often when people are brought to this stillness for the first time, they think they cannot pray any longer, because they cannot form words, but this prayer is deeper than words. The spirit is able to commune with God without saying anything, just as lovers are able to do when their relationship matures. The Curé d'Ars, a great French saint of the last century, was curious to know what an old peasant man was doing when he came and sat in the church in silence every day. When he asked him what he was doing, the old man replied, 'I look at him, and he looks at me, and we understand one another.' That is the essence of contemplation.

In previous times of the Church's history it was often thought that contemplation was for monks and nuns, who had given up their secular life and were entirely given to the religious life. The monasteries kept the tradition of contemplation alive when it almost completely died out in the Western Church.

In the Eastern Orthodox Churches, however, there has always been a tradition of contemplation amongst lay people. It has never died out in parish life. But in our day the gift and practice of contemplative prayer is coming back into the prayer life of lay people leading secular lives in the Western Churches also. This can cause problems in parishes where there is no understanding of this kind of prayer, but the monasteries and convents are a resource for lay contemplatives where they can find help and spiritual direction.

In recent times the religious houses in the West have opened themselves up as places where lay people can go for retreats, quiet days and spiritual direction. The retreat movement is one of the growth areas in the Church, because of the demand of lay people for spiritual help in their prayer life, but particularly because of the recent growing interest in the practice of contemplation.

It is good to start a time of contemplation with a meditation which will lead us into contemplation and help us to focus our mind on God. Then it may be necessary to have some symbol before our eyes to keep us focused – a lighted candle, a cross, a piece of God's creation; or a mantra – a word which will bring us back when our mind wanders, such as 'Jesus', 'love', 'God', 'Father' – which we can repeat as necessary. In this time of contemplation we may not be conscious of anything happening at all, but if we practise it regularly, we will find that we are slowly changing – becoming more peaceful and integrated in our personality.

It is rather like going on a flight in an aeroplane. To begin with, the aeroplane has to work hard to get off the ground, but soon it is airborne, and climbing rapidly. Then it reaches the clouds, and for some time you cannot see anything out of the windows except a grey mist. Eventually the mist grows lighter, and then you are above the clouds, bathed in sunlight, with a glittering panorama of white carpet which parts in places to show you glimpses of the world below you.

So it is with contemplation. It may be hard to start with, but once you are used to this kind of prayer, you can 'take off', so to speak. Soon you are into the cloud of unknowing where you cannot see anything at all; you are driving blind through the cloud. If, however, you persevere through the cloud, you find it becoming lighter, until you come out of it into the light of the Son, which illuminates the whole of the spiritual world, and you begin to see spiritual truths and the world as God sees it. When you come down to earth you will find that illuminated as well, and you will begin to see God in all of life.

As in meditation, the Benedictines will aim at balance of mind and spirit in their contemplation, and the Ignatians will include visions and feelings, but the Carmelites aim to go beyond pictures and thoughts and feelings into wordless prayer. They also recognize that the times when prayer is tough are times of spiritual growth, and that if we are wise we will welcome the difficult stages as well as the pleasant ones because they are sent not to try but to help us. Many people go through a so-called 'desert' experience, which is a time of stripping from all influences that may be holding us back.

It is like pruning the roses. It means that we will do better as a result; but it is hard being pruned, and we need trust and hope to persevere through these difficult times. This is why it is helpful to have a spiritual director, or soul friend to help us in our spiritual journey – to rejoice with us when God seems to be pouring out his blessing, but also to encourage us when the way is hard. Yet it is through the hard times that we can grow spiritually in a way that we can only really appreciate in hindsight. Jesus never pretended that it would be easy to follow him, but he promises us a great reward. So in our prayer life we can expect difficult times, but a reward beyond our greatest hopes.

That is true of the whole of our prayer life, whether we are natural contemplatives or not. Some people take to this kind of prayer like ducks to water; others find they need practice before they can do it; others find it is not for them at all. If you are not a contemplative, it doesn't mean that you cannot pray, but that you need to find the kind of prayer that is natural to you. The rest of this book will help you to find that.

Exercises

- There are many classics that have been written on contemplation. A good introduction to some of these is the *Enfolded in Love* series published by Darton, Longman and Todd. This series of pocket-sized books presents selected extracts from the spiritual classics in a form suitable for daily reading and meditation. It includes:

  The Dart of Longing Love: Daily Readings from the Cloud of Unknowing, edited by Robert Llewellyn.

  The Desert of the Heart: Daily Readings with the Desert Fathers, edited by Benedicta Ward.

  Enfolded in Love: Daily Readings with Julian of Norwich, edited by Robert Llewellyn.

  Lamps of Fire: Daily Readings with St John of the Cross, edited by Elizabeth Ruth, ODC.

  Living Water: Daily Readings with St Teresa of Avila, edited by Sister Mary.

  Threshold of Light: Prayers and Praises from the Celtic Tradition, edited by A. M. Allchin and Esther de Waal.

- Take a retreat. A good one to go on would be an individually guided retreat (IGR) which is usually Ignatian in style, but there are many to choose from. Advice can be sought from the National Retreat Association – an ecumenical organization which publishes a magazine called *Vision* which contains a list of all the retreats taking place in England, the Channel Islands, Wales, Scotland and Ireland, listed under counties.[1]

- Practise daily a time of meditation followed by contemplation. For the meditation refer to the session on meditation (p. 13) and in addition you could use one of the books referred to in the first exercise above to start you off. The meditation should lead into a time of silence as you get used to this kind of prayer.
- An easy alternative to a retreat for those who find it hard to get away from home is to spend a quiet day in a local convent, monastery or retreat house. You will find a list of these in the magazine, *Vision.*[2] It would be helpful to ask for advice from someone at the retreat house as to how to use the day. Some retreat houses run quiet days; others will allow you to use their facilities if you phone or write beforehand and let them know when you are coming.
- It is often easier to pray the prayer of contemplation with other people in a group. There are networks of contemplative groups in this country that welcome visitors or new members. The Fellowship of Contemplative Prayer[3] uses Scripture as a basis for meditation leading to contemplation.

  Julian meetings are groups that meet for contemplative prayer for those who are attracted to the writings of Mother Julian of Norwich.[4]

17

PRAYING IN THE SPIRIT

To pray in the Spirit means to be Spirit-led in our prayer, and this means yielding up the control of what we do to the Spirit, yielding to his influence, rather than bringing our own concerns in our own way. We need to invoke the Spirit, to ask him to come and fill us and to pray in us in a way that will be pleasing to the Father. He can help us to praise God and to love him in a way that is not possible for us on our own. He can intercede for us and for the world in a way that will go directly to the Father's heart.

St Paul says,

> the Spirit helps us in our weakness. We do not know what we ought to pray for, but the Spirit himself intercedes for us with groans that words cannot express. And he who searches our hearts knows the mind of the Spirit, because the Spirit intercedes for the saints in accordance with God's will. (Romans 8.26–7)

St Paul also says, 'hope does not disappoint us, because God has poured out his love into our hearts by the Holy Spirit, whom he has given us.'[1] It is the Spirit who pours his love into our hearts so that we can love and adore God, and offer him that worship in the Spirit and in truth for which the Father is seeking.

The Spirit also gives us gifts which help us to pray. The best-known of these is the gift of tongues, which is a gift of being able to speak in a language unknown to the speaker, but recognizable to someone who knows that language.

For example, the late Revd Dr Denis Ball used to tell a story of how he was speaking in a hall at the end of a pier. In the interval he wandered out of the hall on to the pier, and hung over the rail praying out loud in tongues, as he thought there was no one near to hear him. But there was a lower deck to the pier beneath him, and a man appeared up some steps and said to him, 'Please tell me more about this Jesus.' Apparently, without knowing what he was saying, or knowing the language, Denis Ball had been speaking in Mandarin Chinese, which was known to the man, who heard him speaking to Jesus, and wanted to know more.

This gift of a language is clearly described in Acts 2.5–11, where the gift of the Holy Spirit to the apostles is followed by the gift of tongues, and all the audience could hear and understand what they were saying because the languages, though unknown to the apostles, were known to the audience which was drawn from all over the Eastern Mediterranean.

The gift of tongues is usually given today to those who have received the 'baptism of the Spirit'; that is those who have been completely filled with the Spirit following a submission to the lordship of Christ in every area of their life. The gift of tongues is not mandatory for Christians, but it is a powerful tool for prayer. It is usually used only for private prayer, and is helpful to employ particularly when it is difficult to know what to pray. The Spirit knows what to pray, however, and the use of tongues enables the Spirit to pray in us in a very powerful way.

Another gift mentioned in 1 Corinthians 12 which helps us to pray is the gift of knowledge, which means to know by supernatural means something we did not know about a person or situation, but which helps us to pray more specifically about them. Closely allied to this is the gift of prophecy, which enables us to hear what God is saying about a situation, rather than foretelling the future. It may be given in the form of a picture or of words, or a passage from Scripture. Both these gifts help us to know what to pray for, and to respond to God's will for us or for a situation.

To receive these gifts and the infilling of the Spirit, it is helpful to ask other Christians who are used to a ministry of laying-on of hands to pray for us, though the gifts and infilling can also come as a result of private prayer. The Church prays for this infilling at baptism and confirmation, and though we receive the Holy Spirit when the Church prays, the recipient is not always ready at that moment to be completely filled with the Spirit because they themselves have not completely given their lives to Christ. God will only work with what we are willing to give to him, and it is only when we are completely willing to allow ourselves to be led by Christ and his Holy Spirit that God is able to lead us as he wills. He will not force us, or coerce. We have to say our 'Yes' to him first. It is as we willingly give the whole of ourselves to him that we receive his gifts. Many people are afraid to let go for fear of what God will ask of them, and it may take some time before enough trust is built up for us to let ourselves go entirely into the hands of God. But it is love to whom we give ourselves, and it is our freedom that we gain when we let go of our self-will.

A Prayer for the Infilling of the Holy Spirit

Lord Jesus,
I give myself to you.
I submit to your leading and guiding.
Please fill me with your Spirit.
Please give me your gifts,
Please fill me with your love,
So that I may love and serve you
And pray according to your perfect will.
Amen

Exercises

- Use Romans 8.26–7 and Romans 5.5 as a focus for your meditation. Then say the prayer for the infilling of the Holy Spirit. Ask the Holy Spirit to help you to pray, and have a time of waiting on God. If you have any difficulty, ask for laying-on of hands from someone who has this ministry.
- Use 1 Corinthians 12 as a focus for your meditation. Then say the prayer for the infilling of the Holy Spirit. Ask the Holy Spirit to help you to pray, and to give you whatever of the gifts that you need. After a time of waiting on God, thank him for his Spirit, and for the gifts of the Spirit. Again, if you have any difficulty, ask for laying-on of hands from someone who has this ministry.
- Use Acts 2.1–13 as a focus for your meditation. Then say the prayer for the infilling of the Holy Spirit. Ask the Holy Spirit to help you to pray, and if he wills that he might give you the gift of tongues. After a time of waiting on God, thank him for his Spirit, and for the gift of tongues. Again, if you have any difficulty, ask for laying-on of hands from someone who has this ministry.

18

PRAYING WITH THE HANDS

A vicar of a South London church noticed that something was happening to the men of the congregation who were helping out by cleaning and painting the gutters of the church. They seemed to be experiencing spiritual renewal.

St Benedict, when he composed his *Rule for Monks* in the sixth century, had noticed that work with the hands, when offered to God, had a spiritual effect. He laid down in the Rule that his monks should spend one third of the day in prayer, communal and private; one third in study; and one third working with the hands.

At the beginning of this century, when working with mentally handicapped children, Dr Maria Montessori found that exercises with the hands had a therapeutic effect. When she tried out the exercises she had devised with normal children, the effect was startling. They became more integrated mentally and spiritually, learned how to concentrate, and all aggressive or disruptive behaviour ceased.

There is something about work with the hands which enables us to achieve an integration of the whole person – physical, mental and spiritual – and become what in prayer terms we would call being 'recollected'. Something like gardening, which engages the whole person, can bring us closer to God as we work with his creation. Even doing the more humdrum tasks, such as washing-up, can be times when we can pray more easily. Many people who find it hard to pray when they kneel down or sit still to do so can pray if they are working with their hands in a menial job. The operative thing seems to be that we need to offer whatever we are doing to God, to release the spiritual dimension in us as we work. George Herbert, in his hymn 'Teach me, my God and King', expresses this perfectly.

> Teach me, my God and King,
> In all things thee to see;
> And what I do in anything
> To do it as for thee.
>
> A man that looks on glass,
> On it may stay his eye;

Or, if he pleaseth, through it pass,
And then the heaven espy.

All may of thee partake;
Nothing can be so mean
Which, with this tincture, 'For thy sake',
Will not grow bright and clean.

A servant with this clause
Makes drudgery divine,
Who sweeps a room, as for thy laws,
Makes that and the action fine.

This is the famous stone
That turneth all to gold;
For that which God doth touch and own
Cannot for less be told.

Recreational work with the hands, such as painting, can also have this effect. A very successful series of retreats with the theme of painting and prayer was started by Canon Charles Shells, and is now run regularly at retreat houses all over the country. You do not need to be an expert or talented painter to take part, only to enjoy painting. Many find this a relaxing kind of retreat that helps them to pray.[1] In addition to painting and prayer retreats, calligraphy, embroidery, music appreciation, poetry and creative writing retreats have been introduced as successful variants of the original concept.[2]

Those going on a Benedictine retreat[3] with Esther de Waal or others will find themselves doing some manual work such as preparing vegetables, mending curtains, or whatever jobs the retreat house warden has been saving up!

All of us have to do some form of manual work at some time. Offered to God this can be a form of prayer. For some people who think that they cannot pray because they cannot sit still for any length of time this can be a liberation. For those who have to do manual work such as housework or gardening, to turn it into prayer can take away the drudgery of it. For those with busy lives, those times when we are washing-up or cleaning can be a window on to our prayer life if offered to God. Follow the Benedictine rule and pray with your hands!

Exercises

- Find a task which you have to do with your hands. Offer it to God, and then use the time when you are doing it to draw close to God and pray to him.
- Find a recreational task you can do with your hands such as painting, embroidery, writing, etc. Offer the task to God, and use the time to draw near to God in your recreation and pray to him.
- Find a manual task, such as cleaning the church or churchyard, or helping an elderly or sick neighbour in the house or garden. Offer the task to God, and use the time to draw near to him and pray to him for the church or for the neighbour.

19

MYSTICAL PRAYER

The essence of mystical prayer is that it is directed towards union with God. One cannot decide to become a mystic, but individuals are called into this closest union with God that is called the 'spiritual marriage'. It involves a total stripping of all that would hinder the person on this path so that they can be totally given to God. Some people are called to friendship with God, but this is a closer union of the lover with the beloved. It cannot be expressed except by the allegory of marriage.

The prayer is an 'infused' prayer; that is to say it is given by God, and not something that can be worked on. It is given, usually, only to certain of those who are called to be contemplatives and have been living a contemplative life over a number of years. The mystic is caught up into contemplation – which is loving and being loved by God – into adoration of him, and eventually into union with him.

This union is not the end of the road, but the beginning. The mystic is then usually sent out into the world and involved in building community or serving society in some way. It has been said that everything begins in mysticism and ends in politics. It is true that many inspired activities have come this way. Certainly it can be seen by studying the lives of well-known mystics such as St Francis and St Catherine of Siena that they had a tremendous impact on the society of their day. Few are called to have the intense experiences or the profound impact on society of a St Francis, but there is a sense in which everyone who deepens their prayer life reflects something of this calling to come closer into God so as to go out in the strength of God into the world.

Coming apart to be with God is not a self-indulgence or a self-seeking; it is coming closer to the reality of all that is. It is often the hermits who have the clearest idea of what is going on in society and have their finger on the pulse of it. And those who have been 'in the desert' with God in solitude are those who generally give the grace they have received back to society in some form or other.

This movement into God and out into the world is the ebb and flow of our prayer life, which should enrich everything that we do in community. What we do in our time of prayer influences our life in the world, and vice versa. Prayer and action are two sides of one coin. The deeper we go into God, the more profound the impact on our lives and the lives of others will be. As we go deeper into the life of God, we will find ourselves being drawn to those who are in pain in our community; those who need to be reconciled to God and one another; those who need God's love particularly. We will be called to help to build up Christian community, and to influence the wider society in which we are set. So our prayer life is not an end in itself, though we should seek God for himself alone. It is the giving and receiving of a love which is always seeking to extend God's kingdom, to build family and community, and to reconcile and heal in a hurting world.

Jesus shows this ebb and flow of life lived in union with God and yet drawn into an intense ministry of teaching, preaching and healing. There are the hidden years in Nazareth when the foundations of his ministry were being laid. At the beginning of his three years' ministry, he spends forty days alone in the desert before he comes into Galilee announcing the good news of the forgiveness of sins. During his ministry he frequently goes apart in solitude or with a few disciples to pray. Before the climax to his three years' ministry, the crucifixion and resurrection, he withdraws up a mountain and experiences the transfiguration. He cannot stay there, however, and is drawn by the Spirit down the mountain into ministry again.

As we follow Jesus, and go deeper into the life of prayer, we will find this pattern establishing itself in our lives. Everyone has their own individual calling, but when God touches our lives we are either prepared for or involved in some way in the work of God's kingdom. Just as the union of two people is the beginning of the establishment of a family, so our partnership with God is the beginning of the establishment of new community, the community of God's kingdom; where God's will is done.[1]

Exercises

- Read the account of Jesus' desert experience in Matthew 4.1–11 followed by 4.12–17. Use it as a meditation out of which to make your own prayer.
- Read the account of the transfiguration in Matthew 17.1–13. Use it as a meditation out of which to make your own prayer.

- Review your life at the moment – your prayer life and your active life. In your prayer life, are you conscious of drawing closer to God? In your active life, are you conscious of God giving you opportunities to minister to those in need? Or to build family or community? Meditate on your answer to these questions and out of the meditation make your own prayer.

Transfiguration

The last rays of the setting sun
Tint the clouds with pink and gold.
Glastonbury Tor is etched in steel blue
Against a deep pink sky.
A golden light invests the landscape
With an ethereal other-worldly glow
Like an Old Master painting.
The rose-tinted rays of the sun
Turn the golden walls of the cottage
Into a glowing apricot colour.
For a perfect moment the scene is transformed
Into a magic romantic landscape
Reflecting a more heavenly world.
Then the sun drops behind the clouds,
The walls assume a yellow ochre colour,
The landscape loses its lustre,
The moment of transfiguration has gone.
The moment does not last,
The everyday takes over quickly,
But the glimpse of glory remains,
A picture in the mind
That haunts the memory still.

20

PRAYING WITH OTHERS

In Matthew 18.19–20 Jesus says, 'I tell you that if two of you on earth agree about anything you ask for, it will be done for you by my Father in heaven. For where two or three come together in my name, there am I with them.' This may explain why there always seems to be a greater strength or power in our prayer when we come together in a group to pray, whatever kind of group it may be – an intercession group, a contemplative group, or a Bible Study group that prays at the end of the meeting.

On the other hand, there is a certain restraint or artificiality about group prayer which we do not find in our private prayer because we have to fit in with what the group is doing or saying. The group needs to follow a theme which is directed by the Holy Spirit.

There are different styles of group meetings. One is the evangelical style of prayer group, where people pray spontaneously out loud. It is important in a group such as this to follow on from what the previous person has been saying, so that a theme develops in the praying, avoiding disconnected contributions from people present. If they listen to the Holy Spirit and to each other, the Holy Spirit will orchestrate the meeting so that a theme emerges.

Members of intercession groups should be encouraged by Matthew 18.19 to agree about what they want to ask for, and then claim Jesus' promise to honour their prayer. Such groups can either be of the evangelical type with the prayer spoken out, or of the more silent kind, with discussion at the beginning as to what the group wants to pray for, followed by a time of silence in which the prayer is offered.[1]

It is usually much easier to contemplate in a group that is contemplating together. On our own we can struggle and find it hard to concentrate, but in a group the power of the prayer is such that it carries us along, and half an hour of silence can speed by like a few minutes. It is advisable to have some input at the beginning to help people to focus on God.

The Julian meetings[2] start with a brief reading which leads into half an hour of silent prayer. After the silent prayer there is prayer in words or music to give a short coming-out period. The meeting may end with coffee and conversation.

As Jesus says, 'two or three' are all that you need to start a prayer group. If there is no prayer group in your area, you can simply ask a Christian friend or neighbour to pray with you, or you can start your own prayer group, or join a neighbouring prayer group. You will certainly find it worth while. Sometimes prayer groups come together on a temporary basis, such as to pray for a mission that the local church may be having. However the group has been set up, it is an opportunity to get together with other Christians, and as the body of Christ to pray in his name.

Family prayers seem to be something that is going out these days. A friend found that their family prayers were getting shorter and shorter as the children grew up and became more rebellious. But those married couples who pray together value this time very much indeed. A couple in full-time ministry who pray together every morning find that if they miss it for any reason they feel the lack of it acutely. They read the Bible lessons set for the day; then after a time of meditation they pray for each other and for anything that has come out of the readings. Then they intercede for those who have asked for their prayers.

Couples who both work in secular jobs find it more difficult to pray together. The only answer seems to be to set the alarm so that they get up a bit earlier each day, to pray briefly then, and again at night when the children are in bed. Even this short prayer can make all the difference to life and to the day.

Whatever kind of lifestyle you have, and whatever kind of prayer you practise, there is a prayer group for you either already existing, or waiting to be started up. It will strengthen you own prayer life and encourage you on your spiritual journey.

Exercise

- Join an already existing prayer group, or ask a friend to pray with you. Use Matthew 18.19–20 to start with. Decide with your friend beforehand whether you want to use a time of silence. There are three models given in this session suggesting how you could use the time. End with a time of praise and thanksgiving.

21

WORSHIP

To 'worship God' means literally to 'give God his worth'. To worship we can use any or all of the different kinds of prayer described in this part of the book, but particularly we need to praise, thank and adore him. We praise him for his greatness; we thank him for his goodness; we adore him for his love.

We worship him as Creator, our Maker. Jesus tells us that every one of the hairs on our head is numbered. 'It is he who made us, and we are his.'[1] He is Lord of all creation and has made all things well. We also worship him as Redeemer. When mankind had fallen away from God and the world with them, God sent his Son to bring us back again and restore us once more. It is in him that our sins are forgiven and we are made whole. We also worship him as Sustainer, the Lord of all life. It is his Spirit that keeps us in being and brings us to everlasting life – a life that will outlast our present existence. So he sustains us in being in this life and in the life to come.

To worship we can sing as well as pray. St Augustine said that to sing was to pray twice! There are many traditional and modern hymns and choruses we can use to worship God, as well as spoken prayers and silent adoration. The psalmist says, 'Worship the Lord with gladness; come before him with joyful songs.'[2] To worship is a natural instinct in mankind. We all worship something, though it is not always God.

A newscaster spoke of a football crowd as standing outside their place of worship – the football ground. Some people worship their car; some their family. There is nothing wrong with football, or cars, or families, but it is a case of giving our priority where it is due. If we put our worship in God first, then everything else will take its proper place in our life. 'You shall have no other gods before me,' says God to the Israelites in the desert. 'You shall not bow down to them or worship them.'[3]

Worship is something we need to give to God first and foremost. It is what we have been made to do, and the visions of heaven in the book of Revelation show us that it is what we will be doing in heaven also. We hear that the angels standing around the throne fell down on their faces before the throne and worshipped God, saying: 'Amen! Praise and glory and wisdom and thanks and honour and power and strength be to our God for ever and ever. Amen.'[4] To worship like the angels, we need like them to catch a glimpse, even though through a glass darkly, of God and his great love, compassion and power. This is why the patient watching and waiting and listening are so important, because gradually, imperceptibly even, the light is dawning on us even as we wait, and we catch a glimpse of his glory, which sends us to our knees in worship.

Shout for joy to the Lord, all the earth.
Worship the Lord with gladness;
come before him with joyful songs.
Know that the Lord is God.
It is he who made us, and we are his;
we are his people, the sheep of his pasture.

Enter his gates with thanksgiving
and his courts with praise;
give thanks to him and praise his name.
For the Lord is good and his love endures for ever;
his faithfulness continues through all generations.

(Psalm 100)

Hymn

O worship the Lord in the beauty of holiness.
Bow down before him, his glory proclaim;
With gold of obedience, and incense of lowliness,
Kneel and adore him, the Lord is his name.

Low at his feet lay thy burden of carefulness,
High on his heart he will bear it for thee,
Comfort thy sorrows, and answer thy prayerfulness,
Guiding thy steps as may best for thee be.

Fear not to enter his courts in the slenderness
Of the poor wealth thou wouldst reckon as thine:
Truth in its beauty, and love in its tenderness,
These are the offerings to lay on his shrine.

These, though we bring them in trembling and fearfulness,
He will accept for the name that is dear;
Mornings of joy give for evenings of tearfulness,
Trust for our trembling and hope for our fear.

J. S. B. Monsell (1811–75)

Chorus

Hallelujah, my Father
for giving us your Son;
sending him into the world
to be given up for men,
knowing we would bruise him
and smite him from the earth.
Hallelujah, my Father,
in his death is my birth;
Hallelujah, my Father,
in his life is my life.

(Extract from the song by Tim Cullen.

A Modern Psalm for Worship

All blessing and glory and honour and praise
Be to the Father and the Son and the Holy Spirit.
For in love the whole world was created,
And for love we are made.
Listen all created things,
The Father has spoken through the Son,
And given him all things for his dominion.
God has made all things well,
And redeemed us through his Son.
He has given us his Holy Spirit
To lead and guide us in the way,
so that we should not stumble or fall,
But serve him in holiness all our days.
Blessed be God the Father, Maker of all things,
Blessed be God the Son, Redeemer of the world,
Blessed be God the Holy Spirit, Sustainer of all life.
All blessing and glory and honour and praise
Be to the Father and the Son, and the Holy Spirit
Now and for evermore.

Amen

Exercises

- Meditate on God as your Maker, using the words from Psalm 100, but making it personal by saying: 'It is he that has made me, and I am his.' Out of your meditation make an act of worship to the God who made you, who saw you and knew you in the womb, and every day since.
- Meditate on God as your Redeemer, using the chorus, 'Hallelujah, my Father'. He has died for you on the cross, so that you may be restored, your sins be forgiven, and you made whole. Out of your meditation make an act of worship to the God who redeemed you, who paid the debt you owed, who has won forgiveness and wholeness for you.
- Meditate on God as Sustainer, keeping your very life in being, using the words from the modern psalm,

  He has given us his Holy Spirit
  To lead and guide us in the way,
  So that we should not stumble or fall,
  But serve him in holiness all our days.

  Out of your meditation make an act of worship to the God who keeps you in being, and who will bring you to everlasting life.
- Read slowly the passages, poems, hymns and psalms quoted in this session, and meditate on anything that particularly strikes you or speaks to you. Make an act of worship using one of the pieces.

Epilogue

SPIRITUAL DIRECTION

'I wish everyone could have another Christian to help them on their spiritual journey,' said a nun who is a spiritual director to me. We all need help, guidance and encouragement on the way, and it is good to have someone to talk to about the difficulties and the rewards of journeying with God.

There are different ways of describing the role of spiritual director: soul friend or spiritual guide. A soul friend is someone you can share with, but who isn't necessarily someone who has the knowledge to guide you. We need someone who is experienced in spiritual matters, who can give us guidance and who can explain what is happening to us. For example, someone whom I met at the Julian Shrine had been drawn into contemplation without knowing what it was, and had been given a charismatic experience without knowing what it was. She was fortunate enough to find a spiritual director through her church, who then had the role of explaining to her what God was doing in her life.

There are also many blocks that we can meet with in our prayer life that we may need help to overcome. For example, many people try too hard when they endeavour to pray. They try to do it themselves instead of letting God pray through them. They try to be too complicated instead of praying simply, or they may be copying someone else's kind of prayer instead of making it their own.

St Ignatius was a natural psychologist, and he knew that we need to know we are loved by God before we can love him in return. In his *Spiritual Exercises*, he starts with praying for a felt experience of God's love before anything else is attempted. This is right, because we need to know, not just believe, that God loves us no matter what we have done or what we are. When we realize that we are loved, then we can begin to respond to God. Again, it is helpful to have someone to pray with or who can minister this felt experience of God's love to us.

We also may need help if we are called into contemplation. This may begin by an inability to pray in words, though we are drawn to God. Many people think that they cannot pray any longer because they can no longer form prayers in words, but on the contrary it means that they are being called deeper into prayer, and need to go with what God is doing. It will be very helpful at this stage to talk to someone who is already a contemplative.

One very common block is a lack of forgiveness. We cannot progress in the kingdom of God if we are nursing any grudges, however well-founded they may be. We receive forgiveness of our sins on only one condition: that we forgive the sins of others. If we are tempted to unforgiveness, we need only to ask God to make us willing to forgive, and to let go of the whole matter into his hands, but until we do this we will not progress in our prayer life. Again it is helpful to have someone who can pray with us about it, and help us to forgive as we have been forgiven.

Above all, we need encouragement to keep on keeping on with prayer. We need to pray whether we feel like it or not, whether we think we are getting anything out of it or not. It is only in the long term that we will be able to see what God is doing with us in our time of prayer, or to regret what is going awry if we cease from prayer. The only time when it is right to rest from prayer is when we feel tired or unwell, but then we need to ask for the prayers of others for help and healing. A spiritual guide can help us through the ups and downs to persevere in our prayer life, so that we can grow and develop in our relationship with God.

There has been an explosion in demand for spiritual direction, so it is not always easy to find someone to walk with you as a fellow pilgrim on the journey. But the National Retreat Association has someone in your area who can help you to find a spiritual director.[1]

Hymn

Jesus, good above all other,
Gentle child of gentle mother;
In a stable born our brother,
Give us grace to persevere.

Lord, in all our doings guide us;
Pride and hate shall ne'er divide us;
We'll go on with you beside us,
And with joy we'll persevere.

J. M. Neale (1816–66)
and Percy Dearmer (1867–1936)

Notes

Chapter 2 Finding Space for God

1. Matthew 6.6.
2. Matthew 6.7–8.
3. Matthew 6.14–15.
4. Mark 11.25.
5. 1 Corinthians 10.13.
6. 1 Corinthians 10.12.

Chapter 3 Focusing on God

1. John 8.12.

Chapter 4 Come to the Father

1. 1 John 4.9.

Chapter 5 Through the Son

1. John 3.35.
2. John 5.19–20.
3. John 10.30.

Chapter 6 By the Power of the Holy Spirit

1. 2 Corinthians 1.21.

Chapter 8 Listening to God

1. John 10.27.

Chapter 10 Petition

1. Matthew 7.7.

Chapter 11 Intercession

1. James 5.16.
2. For more details of Crosswinds, write to Crosswinds, PO Box 1041, Nailsen, N. Somerset BS19 2SD.

Chapter 15 Prayer of the Heart

1. Matthew 13.15.
2. Matthew 15.19.
3. Matthew 5.8.

Chapter 16 Contemplation

1. The National Retreat Association, The Central Hall, 256 Bermondsey Street, London SE1 3UJ; telephone: 0171 357 7736.
2. *Vision* magazine is available from The National Retreat Association, The Central Hall, 256 Bermondsey Street, London SE1 3UJ; telephone: 0171 357 7736.
3. For further information about the Fellowship of Contemplative Prayer, contact Mrs Maxine Nicholas, 1 Weydown Court, Weydown Road, Haslemere, Surrey GU27 1BT, enclosing a stamped addressed envelope.
4. For further information about Julian meetings, contact Mrs Gail Ballinger, The Parsonage, Sambourne Lane, Sambourne, Redditch, Worcs. B96 6PA, enclosing a stamped addressed envelope.

Chapter 17 Praying in the Spirit

1. Romans 5.5.

Chapter 18 Praying with the Hands

1. For details of Painting and Prayer with Theme retreats, send a large

stamped addressed envelope to the Membership Secretary, Dept TV, 182 High Street, Street, Somerset BA16 0NH.

2. For details of other retreats involving creative handwork, see Chapter 18, Note 1, or look in *Vision* magazine, available from The National Retreat Association, The Central Hall, 256 Bermondsey Street, London SE1 3UJ; telephone: 0171 357 7736, or from any retreat house.
3. For details of Benedictine retreats, see *Vision* magazine as in Chapter 18, Note 2.

Chapter 19 Mystical Prayer

1. Further reading on mystical prayer: Sister Frances Teresa, OSC, *Living with the Incarnation* and *Praying with Francis and Clare of Assisi*, Darton, Longman and Todd.

Chapter 20 Praying with Others

1. A list of silent prayer groups is available from The National Retreat Association, The Central Hall, 256 Bermondsey Street, London SE1 3UJ; telephone: 0171 357 7736.
2. For information about Julian meetings, contact Mrs Gail Ballinger, The Parsonage, Sambourne Lane, Sambourne, Redditch, Worcs. B96 6PA, enclosing a stamped addressed envelope.

Chapter 21 Worship

1. Psalm 100.3.
2. Psalm 100.2.
3. Exodus 20.3–4.
4. Revelation 7.12.

Epilogue: Spiritual Direction

1. For a spiritual director, write to or phone the National Retreat Association, The Central Hall, 256 Bermondsey Street, London SE1 3UJ; telephone: 0171 357 7736.

The Society for Promoting Christian Knowledge (SPCK) has as its purpose three main tasks:

- **Communicating the Christian faith in its rich diversity**
- **Helping people to understand the Christian faith and to develop their personal faith**
- **Equipping Christians for mission and ministry**

SPCK Worldwide serves the Church through Christian literature and communication projects in over 100 countries. Special schemes also provide books for those training for ministry in many parts of the developing world. SPCK Worldwide's ministry involves Churches of many traditions. This worldwide service depends upon the generosity of others and all gifts are spent wholly on ministry programmes, without deductions.

SPCK Bookshops support the life of the Christian community by making available a full range of Christian literature and other resources, and by providing support to bookstalls and book agents throughout the UK. SPCK Bookshops' mail order department meets the needs of overseas customers and those unable to have access to local bookshops.

SPCK Publishing produces Christian books and resources, covering a wide range of inspirational, pastoral, practical and academic subjects. Authors are drawn from many different Christian traditions, and publications aim to meet the needs of a wide variety of readers in the UK and throughout the world.

The Society does not necessarily endorse the individual views contained in its publications, but hopes they stimulate readers to think about and further develop their Christian faith.

For further information about the Society, please write to:
SPCK, Holy Trinity Church, Marylebone Road,
London NW1 4DU, United Kingdom.
Telephone: 0171 387 5282